# Creative Prayer

# Creative Prayer

Chris Tiegreen

SPEAKING THE LANGUAGE OF GOD'S HEART

MULTNOMAH
BOOKS

CREATIVE PRAYER
PUBLISHED BY MULTNOMAH BOOKS
12265 Oracle Boulevard, Suite 200
Colorado Springs, Colorado 80921
*A division of Random House Inc.*

ISBN 978-1-59052-931-7

Library of Congress Cataloging-in-Publication Data
Tiegreen, Chris.
       Creative prayer / Chris Tiegreen.
          p. cm.
       Includes bibliographical references.
       ISBN 978-1-59052-931-7
    1. Prayer—Christianity.  2. Creation (Literary, artistic, etc.)—Religious aspects—
    Christianity.  I. Title.
    BV210.3.T53 2007
    248.3'2—dc22

                             2007000879

Printed in the United States of America
2007—First Edition

10 9 8 7 6 5 4 3 2 1 0

Contents

One of my greatest desires in writing a book, especially this one, is to conform carefully to biblical truth without conforming rigidly to traditional expressions of it. The first part of that desire depends on the feedback of others, the second part on their encouragement. I deeply appreciate those who offered their input after reading the manuscript or hearing me speak on the topic of creative prayer, including my wife, Hannah; my co-workers at Walk Thru the Bible; my friends at Daystar Fellowship; and members of the Multnomah team who contributed their expertise and enthusiasm to this project. They have all demonstrated a rare balance in the body of Christ, between conformity where it matters and freedom where it doesn't. I'm extremely grateful for that.

# A PERSONAL APPROACH TO GOD

There once was a young man who was deeply, passionately, zealously, joyfully in love with a young woman. Every time he saw her, his heart leaped with exhilaration and hopefulness. He knew—absolutely *knew,* beyond the shadow of a doubt—that she was the perfect match for him. If ever a guy was smitten, captivated, whipped, or any other word that describes consuming passion, it was this man. He loved her with the best of all possible loves.

He took such delight in her that he could never refrain from communicating his love. He gave her gifts, painted pictures, wrote poems, sang songs, danced, cooked meals, gathered flowers, and described his overwhelming love in the most beautiful words—though words often seemed horribly insufficient. The feelings of his heart constantly flowed forth. He could not keep silent.

The young woman loved the young man too. She adored him, in fact. She received his gifts, his words, and his creative expressions with joy—even when she didn't exactly understand them. And she also frequently expressed her feelings to him. How? She told him how she felt, albeit briefly and usually by cell phone. Just words. No gifts, except on holidays. No paintings, songs, dances, or poems. No meals and no flowers. Just talk.

The problem in this relationship, of course, had nothing to do with a lack of love. It was entirely about communication. The young man let his love overflow in every kind of expression—his voice, his service, his talents, his visual creativity. And she communicated with him only one way: through talking to him.

That's an unbalanced relationship, but it's an accurate picture of the way many of us communicate with God. He speaks to us from the love of his heart with pictures, symbols, music, scenery, tastes, sounds of nature, smells of plants and incense and rain, and the soft, gentle caresses of the wind, of the waves, and of other human beings. And how do we express ourselves to him? For most of us, during a disciplined time each morning or evening. And it's usually nothing more than words.

Our words can be very heartfelt. But considering the multidimensional ways in which God communicates with us, spoken language is desperately one dimensional. It offers an extremely limited expression of our hearts.

Think about that. How did God express himself to people in the Bible? His revelation came through the real experiences of people who saw visions, had dreams, and interacted with him through the physical elements of life. God gave a rainbow to Noah, a ladder to Jacob, a burning bush to Moses, an ark and a tabernacle to Israel, a giant to David, a marriage to Solomon and his beloved, a family to Isaiah, figs to Jeremiah, dry bones to Ezekiel, a wife to Hosea, a vine to Jonah, and horsemen to Zechariah and John—to name a few. His voice has come in the sound of thunder, a waterfall, singing, a fire, a wind, a gentle whisper, and more. God expresses himself in terms of fragrance, sound, touch, taste, and anything else our senses can take in.

*Real love—or real emotions
of any kind—can't be contained.*

This book will make the case that real love—or real emotions of any kind—can't be contained. Words aren't enough to express them. Corporately as a church, we're pretty good at creating music and liturgical art to express ourselves to God, but there's so much more for us to do—especially as individuals. Real love is irrepressible and comes out in many, many ways. By its very nature, it's creative.

Before we get into the specifics about creative prayer, I need to be clear about what these words mean in this book. By creative, I'm not talking about the kind of creation that only God can do. Genesis uses two words for God's creative work: *bara* and *asah*. *Bara* means "to create" something out of nothing, and no human being or other created being is able to do that. Only God can. He certainly allows us the privilege of partnering with him by praying for the new creation, but I'm aware that this is a partnership, not a unilateral ability of humanity to create something out of nothing. In other words, this book is *not* an attempt to deify human beings.

*Asah* means "to make" something out of material that already exists. In Genesis 1, for example, God created *(bara)* the heavens and the earth, but he made *(asah)* the expanse, sun, moon, and stars. On the seventh day, God rested from all that he had created *(bara)* and made *(asah)*.[1] Bible translations often use these words interchangeably, sometimes translating *bara* as "made" and *asah* as "created," but they are fundamentally different.

Human beings do not *bara* anything, so when we discuss *creative* prayer, we're talking about the common usage of the word today: imaginative, artistic, original, visionary, and so on. We're also, at times, talking about the power of prayer as a partnership with God in the new creation. I use the words *create* and *creative* broadly and imprecisely in this book because we use them broadly and imprecisely in modern English.

> *Prayer refers to the two-way communication we have personally with God.*

I also use the word *prayer* very broadly and imprecisely. We frequently think of prayer as asking God for something, and it certainly includes that. But it also includes praising God, thanking him, and listening to him. In this book, it refers generally to the two-way communication we have personally with God. That two-way communication happens in a lot of ways, and we will use *prayer* to describe all of them. Think of the subject as "a creative prayer life," if that helps.

Though this book will discuss human creativity extensively, the point is not simply to encourage more creative expression. The world has quite a bit of that already. Neither is the point to encourage more creative expression *about* God. The church has quite a bit of that already too, all throughout its history. The purpose of this book is to discuss creative expression *to* God, to let our interaction with him overflow with our whole personality—emotions, artistry, and everything else he has put within us. After all, that's how God communicates: like a young man madly in love with his sweetheart, unwilling to confine his love to mere words.

One

# THE BREATH OF LIFE

## God Is Not a Formula

ong, long ago, our planet was shrouded in darkness. It was a mysterious chaos, a completely unordered mass of raw material. There were no plants, no seasons, no dry land, no light. "Formless and void," Scripture describes it. Shapeless and empty. Confused and meaningless. Deep and dark. Desperately lifeless.

But a Spirit brooded over the deep. As a wind caressed the waters, he blew away the darkness and hovered over the surface of chaos, contemplating his design and breathing the Breath of meaning into the emptiness.[2] The Hebrew word means "to hover, to move, to brood."[3] His movement was a mission of fertility, and soon this formless mass exploded in creativity. The shapeless raw material became beautiful.

Not long after, God formed the shape of a man out of the dust of the ground. Genesis says he breathed his own Breath into this lifeless being; face-to-face and mouth to mouth, the divine Spirit awakened humanity—the pinnacle of creation. The first sensation this new creature felt was the warm Breath of a creative God; the first thing he saw was God's face. His surroundings were already lush with life and fruit, stunning in beauty, and perfectly suited to sustain the created order. The Master had painted, sculpted, written, and orchestrated wonder and majesty into his work. The Breath that hovered, the Wind of God, was powerful, perfect, and extremely imaginative.[4]

Adam didn't rise up into life to see a blueprint, to hear an explanation, or to find a matrix of complex codes. He awoke to find pictures and sounds and scents and tastes, to feel the warmth of the Breath and the cool of the breeze, and to have those sensations laid out in a progression of time so he could witness the interplay of creation. This Spirit that brooded had not painted by numbers or followed an instruction manual. God thought "outside the box" in everything he did. He didn't even have a box to think outside of.

> God thought "outside the box" in everything he did.

The first couple, we are told, had been made in the image of God—the God whose Spirit hovered and breathed. They had been entrusted with a taste of the Creator's creativity, blessed with a reflection of his imagination. They would have the ability to create using the tools and raw materials God had given them, and there would be almost no limit to the ways they could express themselves.

Why did God create people in his image? Over the course of Scripture, the answer becomes obvious. We were made in the image of God in order to relate to him. We each have a mind, a will, emotions, a voice, facial expressions, gestures—everything we need to communicate at a personal level. And, because the One we relate to is highly imaginative, we have the ability to do it creatively.

But human potential took a nasty fall when the first couple gave in to temptation, and we know the tragic result. The God who made them came to them in the Garden—in "the cool of the day," most translations say, though it's literally "the Breath of the evening," in the Spirit who had hovered and exhaled life into the chaos—and they hid. They had no urge to communicate, to relate to their Creator as they were designed to do. Expression turned inward as they suppressed themselves in hiding.

Creativity took an ugly turn after that. We read of the son of a murderer who became the father of "all those who play the lyre and pipe." Another son of the same murderer was the father of those who forge bronze and iron.[5] And for millennia, the creative breath of humanity sang music to false gods, crafted hand-carved idols, and designed offensive atrocities like the tower of Babel in an attempt to become divine. Human ingenuity and expression didn't cease; it just got really, really twisted.

*Human ingenuity and expression didn't cease; it just got really, really twisted.*

We get a glimpse of restoration much later when God led his people out of Egypt and into the wilderness. He gave specific instructions to Moses for making the ark of the covenant and the other articles of worship to be used in the tabernacle. And for only the second time since time began, the God of Israel filled a human being directly with his Spirit—that fertile Wind of creativity that once hovered over the deep. Who was it? An artist. Bezalel, or *Btsal'el*, meaning "under the shadow of God." His name is derived from a root word that implies not just shade, but a shadow that *hovers*.

God breathed into Bezalel and (by implication) Oholiab, skilled craftsmen, so they could make a work of art.[6] The New Testament tells us that this work of art—actually a collection of works of art, as the tabernacle included multiple elements—was a copy and shadow of heavenly things.[7] It is exhibit A in the argument that God values physical expressions of invisible realities. Many centuries later, he would incarnate his Son—not just an expression of the invisible, but an embodiment of the eternal One. But the tabernacle in the wilderness reflected the courts of heaven and pointed to the coming of the Son. God commissioned this work of art because inward truths are to be expressed outwardly.

That's a major statement from the Lord of a now dark and defiled creation. Centuries, even millennia, had passed since the last time he breathed into humanity at the dawning of creation, when a mound of dust was filled with life. Now, at the moment when a covenant of worship was established with a chosen people, he breathed again. Two wood- and metalworkers were gifted with divine creativity. They would craft a highly symbolic picture that would point to redemption, a re-genesis, a new humanity free to express itself to its Creator. Once again, this time spiritually, chaos was being called to order.

So God commissioned these two artists, and flesh was again filled with divine Breath. The box they made, the ark of the covenant, also reflected the pattern: a spiritual reality expressed in created materials. This intersection of God and humanity would be a model of things to come. The mingling of minds and emotions between the eternal and the temporal, the Creator and created, would continue to produce pictures, symbols, sounds of worship, smells of sacrifice, graphic images in prophecies and parables, and much, much more. And none of it—absolutely none of it—would fit a formula.

## A MULTIMEDIA GOD

God is not a formula. That should be obvious to us, though religious instincts have always tried to make him one. But if his varying modes of expression weren't clear to us before the incarnation, they certainly should be now. God showed us plainly how he communicates.

Long ago, this Creator of the universe clothed himself in human flesh and walked our dusty roads. He also ate our food, wore our clothes, lived in our towns, talked to our ancestors, felt our emotions, and experienced all the pain our nervous systems can experience. He lived a thoroughly human life.

> *Long ago, this Creator of the universe clothed himself in human flesh and walked our dusty roads.*

This wasn't the first time our Creator communicated with us, of course. He spoke to our father Abraham in the form of physical messengers; he spoke to Moses in the form of a desert brush fire that didn't destroy the brush; he showed his face in a daytime cloud and a nighttime fire; his voice thundered from a mountain; his angels sent audible instructions to his servants; and his Spirit, his Breath, inspired prophets, priests, and kings to preach, write, and sing.

But when he clothed himself in flesh and walked among us, his communication got much more tangible to a much larger audience.

He gave us concrete examples. We can learn a lot from how the God-man expressed himself to others. His words and actions tell us much about how our Creator interacts with us.

One of the first things we learn about his communication style is that it was extremely varied. Take his healing of the blind, for example. On some occasions, he spoke words of power and authority, and the blind regained their sight.[8] On other occasions, he simply touched them and they were healed.[9] And sometimes he combined spit and dirt and the touch of his hands to restore sight.[10] One such healing even included a bath in the pool of Siloam before blindness left.[11] In this series of nearly identical issues, Jesus expressed himself differently almost every time. He did not relate to people using a formula.

In fact, almost nothing in Jesus' ministry fit a formula. Sometimes he taught with straightforward preaching; other times he used obscure parables. He responded immediately to the faith of one Gentile[12] and played really hard to get with another.[13] On many occasions he was very vocal toward the authorities who opposed him,[14] but at history's most critical moment was absolutely silent toward them.[15] He often waited for people to come to him before helping them; other times, he approached them even when they didn't seem interested.

Throughout the pages of the Gospels, we see a Savior who is simultaneously accessible and elusive, public and private, vocal and silent, complex and simple, profound and plain, never likely to say exactly the same thing to the same people twice. And the ways he communicated ranged from the obvious, like straightforward speech, to the enigmatic, like drawing in the sand, cooking fish on the shore, prophesying in pictures, preaching in parables, cursing a fig tree, dipping his bread with a traitor, walking on water, calming a storm, being illuminated on a mountain, hearing a voice out of heaven, receiving a descending Dove, and eating a somber meal with eternal significance—to name but a few. None of these actions were just routines of the day, the activities that get us from one place to another and accomplish the tasks we need to get done. They were the first-century version of a multimedia event involving sights, sounds, smells, tastes, and touch. They demonstrated a wide range of creative expression. If Jesus had written a book titled *A Savior's Guide to Effective Communication,* it would have no conclusion. It would be open-ended, because he kept varying his style.

His Father has been no less creative throughout the centuries of human existence—and before, for that matter. We don't know all the amazing creatures of heaven, though we're given glimpses in Scripture of living beings with wings, four faces, multiple body shapes, and dazzling light or glorious colors. But we do know of the creativity of God's visible creation: majestic mountains and waterfalls, unfathomable seas, breathtaking shorelines, colorful landscapes, intricate ecosystems, delicate flowers, elaborately designed insects, stunningly beautiful people, and so much more.

But those are just the visual aspects that seem most obvious to us. God has also filled this world with music-making creatures, roaring rapids, the angry thunder of a black sky, and the rhythmic waves of the sea, and he's given us ears that can tune in to these aural wonders. He has created aromas both pleasant and repulsive—and with divinely orchestrated consistency, the pleasant scents lead us to beauty, and the repulsive ones warn of us danger. He has given us textures and temperatures that can make us feel warm and fuzzy, cold and lonely, tired and sore, loved and accepted, and overwhelmed with ecstasy. And the tastes…well, try visiting the array of ethnic restaurants in nearly every major city in the world, and you'll never run out of wonderfully intriguing flavors to sample. The expressions of God in the physical world are uncountable.

His expression in spiritual matters is no less diverse, though we pick up on his voice and actions much less easily there. Even so, we can read about them in our Bibles if we haven't experienced them ourselves. We've already mentioned the rainbow that made a promise to Noah, the burning bush, the thunderous voice, and the glory cloud by day and the pillar of fire by night. Add to that the fire that fell from heaven on Elijah's altar, the aroma of burnt sacrifices and incense in the tabernacle and temple, the blood and bitter herbs of the Passover, the sulfurous smell of judgment, the simple tastes of the supper portraying redemption, and on and on and on.

> *According to Scripture, God is vocal, visual, tactile, and in every other way sensory in his expression.*

The obvious truth is that God, according to Scripture, is vocal, visual, tactile, and in every other way sensory in his expression. He is a creative communicator from Genesis to Revelation. That's easy to see in events like the Exodus and the path to the Promised Land, the worship in the temple, and the cross and resurrection of Jesus, as well as in the graphically visual books of Daniel, Ezekiel, and Revelation. But the imaginativeness of God's expression is discernible everywhere in Scripture, not to mention everywhere in our day-to-day routines, if we're sensitive enough to notice. The libraries of the world couldn't contain all the descriptions of his creativity, and we would never have time to read all those descriptions anyway. But why read about them in the first place? Look around. His personality has a pretty wide range.

## An Emotional God

Where does all this creativity come from? God didn't just invent senses and a full range of emotions. He has them. We know this because he describes himself this way in Scripture. Clearly spelled out on the pages of your Bible is a God who loves passionately, burns with jealousy for those he loves, gets angry, hates all manner of sin, has deep compassion for his people, rejoices with singing, celebrates the return of his prodigals, and accomplishes his will with zeal. God's description of himself conveys an intensity of feeling beyond compare.

That sounds too human for most people; it seems suspiciously like a God made in our own image. We don't understand how he who is not surprised by anything can have swells of feeling that correspond with changing circumstances. He seems in Scripture to react to the events of history and the hearts of human beings. That portrayal makes him awfully vulnerable, not worthy of the omniscience and omnipotence Scripture ascribes to him elsewhere.

So we theologize these emotions out of God, telling ourselves that he describes himself this way so we can understand him on our terms. But if he is describing himself in emotional terms without actually feeling those emotions, he's not helping us understand him; he's guilty of false advertising. The God of truth is portraying himself in a way that isn't true. That's not possible.

No, God's emotions are true and very real. Despite our theologies, the "human" aspects of God didn't originate with us. God has humanlike senses and a full range of emotions not because we've made him in our image; *we* have God-like senses and emotions because he made us in *his* image. As humanistic students of religion, we've reversed the cause and effect, as though we were the beginning and God's feelings were our invention. But finding similarity between the human and the divine isn't as idolatrous as we often make it out to be. In the Bible, God makes the connection himself.

God's creativity springs out of this truth. As a sentient, emotional being, he is very expressive. The diversity of symbols, signs, smells, sounds, and speech in the Bible are evidence of a Being who has to convey his feelings. We who are made in his image can understand that; we have an inner compulsion to express who we are and how we feel. And we exist in a world like ours because God has the same compulsion. Unexpressed emotions are unsatisfying emotions. They have to be let out.

God's urge to share his feelings with us isn't limited to the Bible. He did not stop conveying his thoughts to us when the canon closed. Are we really to believe that after the first century this expressive Deity, filled with passion, love, and resolve, was content to confine his communication to words on a printed page? Not a chance. He still speaks, and he's still creative in the way he does it.

## MONOCHROME TALK WITH A MULTICOLOR GOD

But this is a book about prayer, isn't it? So why are we spending so much time on God's communication with us rather than ours with him? For one thing, listening to God is a huge part of prayer. For another, if we don't understand how he speaks, we can't understand how he hears.

When we don't understand the creativity of God's expression or the emotional fount from which it springs, our prayers get reduced to the spiritual equivalent of a long-distance telephone conversation. We close off our eyes, ears, noses, mouths, and nerve endings from the constant flow of thoughts and feelings coming to us from our

Creator. Instead, we define his mode of communication in terms of quasi-monastic spirituality, or whatever other preconceived principles of piety our minds have constructed. We're like someone who sits in a symphony hall wearing earphones, because we're sure that if God speaks, it's going to be through the channels we've already tuned to, or like someone who visits the art museum and spends most of the time reading the guidebook rather than viewing the masterpieces. God becomes a monophonic recording or a black-and-white exhibit, and while we listen for words and watch for signs, he gushes with the full majesty of his imagination. In the process, we miss a lot.

> *How we perceive God will dictate how we communicate with him.*

How we perceive God will dictate how we communicate with him. That's why it's important to recognize the multifaceted ways he has expressed himself to (and through) his creation, including us. Before we can pray the way we were meant to, we have to understand the way he communicates. We have to get a glimpse of the Technicolor, surround-sound God who comes to us in total sensory experience. Only then can our prayers connect clearly with the One who made us.

## LOST IN LEVITICUS

Pick up any used Bible—even one pored over by a long-faithful saint—and you'll probably find groups of pages less worn than the others. The cleanest pages will likely begin near the end of Exodus and extend through most of Deuteronomy.

It's no mystery why even earnest Bible students skim over this section of Scripture. It's a labyrinth of obscure prescriptions for rituals and righteousness. It speaks of precise measurements and materials for a tabernacle no longer used; of seemingly endless sacrifices for more occasions than we'll ever encounter; of unpleasant specifics on sores and bodily fluids; and of unspeakable immoral behaviors, unfamiliar dietary restrictions, and inapplicable military censuses. We may begin Genesis with zeal, but zeal turns to determined obedience soon after Exodus 20.

I remember many attempts as a teenager and young adult to read the Bible all the way through. I always began where one should begin, which means I got a good grasp of creation, the patriarchs, and Cecil B. DeMille's most famous script. But the Law beyond the Ten Commandments always boggled my mind.

It's not that I didn't want to understand. I just couldn't. By the time I got into the warp and woof of leprous garments, I was hopelessly lost. I was far removed from the cultural context, and any commentary I found was much too weighty for a guy reared in a sound-bite generation. This portion of God's Word remained inaccessible. Forever inaccessible, it seemed.

But several years ago, I recommitted to reading through all of God's Word again and again. Biographies of spiritual giants of bygone eras reminded me that the Bible was much more understandable in pre-television times. Why? Because understanding the Bible is a matter of spending time in it—reading it, meditating on it, soaking it in, even picturing the events and imagining yourself an eyewitness to them. A fifteen-minute time slot between the sitcom and the baseball game may be enough to catch up on the headlines, but it's not enough to learn the mind of God.

*Understanding the Bible
is a matter of spending time in it.*

So I decided to learn, not by studying word by word, but by imagining thought by thought and event by event. I followed the example of an old missionary I'd read about who spent much time in the Word. He would read each book seven times before moving on. He felt that seven readings was the minimum number by which he could expect to begin to grasp it.

I didn't imitate him exactly, but I followed the principle. And, amazingly, here's what I found: I still didn't understand Leviticus.

Not the outcome you expected, is it? And though it sounds terribly anticlimactic, I kept reading, and a funny thing happened on the way to the Promised Land.

Sometime during a reread of that strange legal document, I began to smell the smell of sacrifice. The vision of a constant stream of blood flowing from the altar began to impact me. The aroma of incense, the sound of bleating, and the hazy air rising from burning flesh filled my disturbed heart. The busy rituals of preparation seemed to say to me over and over again that there once was a vast, tragic rift between me and my God, and there are two things I can never, ever take casually: my sin and his holiness.

The winds of the wilderness and its annoying dust came to symbolize elements of my current environment. The stress of Israel's constant moving yet never arriving explained a lot to me about the human experience. I began to identify with the wandering; it became my story, and the God who guided the wandering with that mysterious cloud and pillar of fire became my God in a new way. He suddenly seemed more frightening yet more familiar, majestic yet merciful, transcendent yet intensely personal, just as he should have seemed all along.

I also came face-to-face with the trauma of fallenness and the crisis of God's presence. I began to understand the weight of this human condition, the drastic distance we had driven ourselves from that pleasant walk in the first Garden. I was reminded that God doesn't just say of our rebellion: "That's okay, I'll take care of it." It's a much bigger deal than that.

Most of all, I found my appreciation deepening for the One who fulfilled this Law, the One who became Israel on our behalf and forever completed this cumbersome covenant. The fact that God cared enough to set up a system for people to relate to him in truth and learn of his holiness—however complicated that system might be—excited me nearly as much as the fact that he satisfied the system himself in our stead. He told us the complex secret for relating to him and then became the complex secret himself, which allowed us to relate to him simply as a Person. He handles the complexity, and we desperately trust him for that. I love that kind of law.

No, I still don't understand all there is to know about Leviticus—or any other part of God's Word, for that matter—and I probably never will, no matter how many commentaries I read. But I feel its weight. I'm certain that every measurement, every material, and every sacrifice is highly symbolic of eternal truths in heavenly places,[16] somehow pointing to the ministry and the cross of Christ. I suspect that some of the Law is perceptible only to the ancient Hebrew mind, and I'm pretty sure that parts of it make sense only in the high courts of heaven.[17] We'll be given further insight into those parts one day when we're allowed to walk the halls of those courts. For now, some legal and Levitical issues remain shrouded in mystery.

I'm okay with that. God never asked my finite little brain to master eternal realities by intellectually dissecting and explaining them. He'd rather I embrace him than decipher him. In a radical departure from my past tendencies, I'm now comfortable with his omniscience and my lack of it. I don't have to explain everything.

*God would rather I embrace him
than decipher him.*

All I know is that somehow as I repeatedly read those mysterious sections of Scripture—and not simply read them, but incorporated into the reading all the sights and smells and sounds implied therein—Leviticus and its obscure companion books came alive. I saw illustrations that have stuck with me. Suddenly, the wisdom of the God of Israel was more profound and majestic than I thought. The depth of the Old Testament shed light on the New. The plan of salvation grew more mysterious and yet more simple. The grace of our Savior became more precious and more worthy of my worship. And certain pages of my Bible are much more worn than they used to be.

To me, this experiment proved that God's communication is more of a spiritual sensory experience than a cognitive process. The alternative to my approach to Leviticus would have been to study the text for syntax and semantics and glean intellectual ideas about the nature of God—something akin to reading a biography of Leonardo da Vinci and describing his personality. But what do we really know about Leonardo if we haven't seen his work? Not much, or at least not much that would actually help us feel a connection with him. Descriptions aren't very personal.

God could have just spoken descriptively of himself rather than being a character in the biographies of his people. He could have given us Scriptures that list an eightfold path or a twelve-step process or a legal code independent of historical context. And we could have come up with our rules and principles from that even more easily than we have from Scripture as it really is.

But clearly God prefers to interact with us at a more personal level. And like any person, he has a multitude of media at his disposal. I found in Leviticus and beyond that his Word was more than his words, that there were snapshots, scents, and soundtracks imbedded in those pages. The Bible, history, circumstances, nature, and the community of faith can become sensory experiences.

## BEYOND FORMULAS

When I lived overseas, I did everything I could to immerse myself in the culture. I studied the language, ate at places few tourists had ever seen, bought clothes at local shops, and adopted gestures and postures that fitted the environment. Why? Because in all my training and preparation, two principles had been drilled into me: (1) effective communication travels through common bonds, and (2) immersion is the key to establishing common bonds.

When "the Word became flesh, and dwelt among us,"[18] God immersed himself in our culture. He spoke our language. But the common bond doesn't end there; we are given new life so we can become citizens of heaven rather than citizens of a fallen world. He adapted to our culture in order to bring us into his. In a sense, the purpose of Scripture is to immerse us in the culture of God, and the Breath that he blows into the redeemed establishes our new citizenship. We become God-filled humans as dramatically as the dust of Eden became a God-filled human.

*In a sense, the purpose of Scripture is
to immerse us in the culture of God.*

As people filled with the Breath of God, we need to learn his language. We need to let ourselves be stretched into the customs and values of heaven, and we can communicate only by expressing a common bond with the Creator. And the only way to do that is to learn that our old formulas don't translate into this new environment. In fact, when it comes to creative expression, none do.

God is not a formula, and I'm glad. An unimaginative builder never would have made the world we live in or hovered over its chaos and rearranged it for beauty. He never would have shaped a pile of dust for a multitextured, multidimensional relationship and breathed the warm Breath of life into it. He would have made a mechanical world, filled it with androids, and set it all in motion. Any variation from programming would be called a problem, not a nice surprise.

Instead, God picked up a heavenly palette and painted this universe in its colors. He sculpted living beings, some of them in his own image, and the Wind of heaven animated them. And for that to mean something—for living beings to be able to relate to him—we had to reflect his personality. We had to be designed for creativity.

# Two

# BORN TO BE WILD

## The Nonconformity of Conforming to Christ

Leonardo da Vinci is considered one of history's greatest, most expressive artists—perhaps even *the* greatest. His artistry was informed not only by his brilliant comprehension of painting and sculpting techniques, but also by his profound understanding of architecture, mechanical engineering, anatomy, biology, mathematics, physics, and astronomy. His mind grasped the movements of water and light better than anyone of his time.

This ability to comprehend nature's dynamics allowed Leonardo to analyze the appearance of things both living and inanimate. He knew how the elements of creation interacted. His imagination was by no means one-dimensional. He is a major reason we call a multitalented and multiskilled person a "Renaissance man."

Leonardo used his artistry for a variety of purposes: to express the religious convictions of the age, to design monuments honoring important people, and to illustrate scientific principles and the structures of nature. He also wrote manuscripts explaining what he had learned. Skilled both as an artist and a writer, his comparison between the two is worth noting. He was a master communicator who understood how abstract concepts and complex ideas are best conveyed. Here's what he said about the effectiveness of writing compared to that of visual art:

> What words can you find, O writer, to equal in your description the complete figure rendered here by drawing? Because of your ignorance of the latter, you have only a confused description and can give only a feeble idea of the true form of things, you are deluded when you think that you can fully satisfy your audience when it comes to evoking a mass enveloped by a surface.
>
> I enjoin you not to encumber yourself with words, unless you address yourself to the blind; if you want to address yourself through words to the ear, and not to the eye, discuss such things as substance and nature; do not trouble yourself with things of the eye, to try and make them pass through the ear; you would be far surpassed in this by painting.
>
> With which words would you describe this heart without filling an entire volume? The more detail you give, the more confusion you will create in your audience, you will need commentaries or references to experience, but in your case there is not much of it, and it touches on only a few aspects of the subject you would encompass completely.[19]

That's a lot of words to explain a simple idea (which, in its own way, proves his point): a picture is worth a thousand words. Actually, Leonardo seemed to believe a picture is worth more than thousands upon thousands of words. There's only so much you can convey through written and spoken language. And when you have the full scene at hand, with all its sights, smells, sounds, tastes, and touch, words really aren't that important anyway. There are much better ways to express truth than by verbal explanation. (Alas, because I did not seem to inherit the artistic ability of my father, a painter and illustrator, you have in your hands a book. It's the best I can do.)

*For most of us, straightforward speech is the only way we speak to God.*

Though the gift of language is one of the key elements of our design—an element we can use rather creatively—it's not our only mode of communication. We've been gifted with many other means of expression. In light of all our options, it seems odd that we pray almost exclusively with words. Audible communication is the one way we expect God *not* to speak to us today—most of us expect him to speak in something other than a booming voice from above. Yet for most of us, straightforward speech is the only way we speak to him. It's an asymmetric relationship. In power and majesty, asymmetry is unavoidable in our bond with him; but when it comes to media of expression, it doesn't need to be. God has equipped us with other, sometimes more powerful, means.

## ONE OF A KIND

In the movie *Pleasantville,* brother and sister David and Jennifer find themselves transplanted into an old television show, where the world is black and white. It's a typical 1950s family show suddenly come to life, where all the messiness of human existence is covered by tidy plots and settings. As David and Jennifer introduce the black-and-white characters of Pleasantville to elements of the real world, the people and scenes of the town gradually turn to color. One by one, the townspeople tap into their true selves whenever they have an authentic human experience. Despite the film's implicit commentary on the benefits of indulging in society's forbidden fruits (the "authentic experience" in the movie is most often sex or some other taboo), it makes a good point: we don't live in color unless we're being real, unless we're able to genuinely express what's in our hearts. Life as an individual is supposed to be…well, individual.

The Bible makes clear that we were fashioned by the Creator individually. God told Jeremiah that he knew the prophet even before he formed him in his mother's womb.[20] David understood that too: "You created my inmost being," he wrote. "You knit me together in my mother's womb."[21] Paul had to remind the church that each member was created and gifted for a singular purpose and had a distinct role in the body.[22] Though Scripture never urges us to be *individualists*—the corporate nature of faith is always a priority— it does affirm that we are *individuals*. The body as a whole depends on having unique members with specific functions.

> *God created us as individuals for a reason.*

God created us as individuals for a reason. If he wanted us to fit a mold, he would have made us from molds. Obviously, he didn't do that. We are unique not only for the sake of one another, but also for his sake. As an infinite Being, he can be worshiped in an infinite number of ways, and there are infinite aspects of his personality to be praised. God created us as individuals because every one of us can worship him in a way that no one else can. For every million believers he has the joy of a million relationships, and no two of them are alike. Our creative God likes the variety.

## SAME MESSAGE, DIFFERENT MESSENGERS

Over the course of the last two millennia, multitudes of creative people have shared a message about Jesus with the rest of us. Some of them have put that message in print; some on canvas; some in songs, hymns, and oratorios; some on film; and some on stage. Within each of those media is a dizzying variety of genres ranging from fictitious parables to accurate scriptural renderings, from somber to whimsical, from simple to elaborate. Within every genre is an even wider range of styles based on the personality, historical context, and purpose of the artist, author, or musician.

To get a glimpse of this range, do a Web search for art on the Annunciation or the Transfiguration, for example, or go to a music store and browse through the CDs in both the contemporary Christian section and the classical religious section. You'll find only a handful of messages about the life and ministry of Christ—granted, they come with limitless emotional gradations and theological nuances—but they all stem from the events recorded in our four Gospels. The messages aren't limitless, but the expression of them is.

*God has a greater appreciation for diversity than anyone who reads our books, views our art, or listens to our music.*

If that's how human creativity expresses messages *about* the life of Jesus to the rest of us, why don't we tap into similar creativity to express our messages *to* him? We're as diverse as we want to be in our person-to-person communication, but very limited in our communication with God—who, ironically, happens to have a greater appreciation for diversity than anyone who reads our books, views our art, or listens to our music. We use our best imagination with the beings we see and withhold it from the One we don't. It doesn't have to be that way.

## CONFORMING TO A NONCONFORMIST

*Diversity* has lately become a highly suspicious word due to how it has been manipulated culturally and politically. Because we live in an "anything goes" society, secular culture interprets God as an "anything goes" God. But God's appreciation for variety doesn't extend beyond the parameters of his character; clearly, in the kingdom of God, not everything "goes." He doesn't compromise who he is for the sake of diversity.

That said, we need to develop a better understanding of his creativity than we currently have. Our natural tendency as social beings is to narrow things down, to push people toward conformity, all for the sake of keeping life manageable. No society has a shortage of norms and expectations. This pressure to conform is, to a degree, healthy and necessary. Sociologists and psychologists call it "socialization."

Most religions take socialization to extremes. We like rules and regulations, written and unwritten, to define what godliness is. We can't be content to say, "Follow Jesus in the power of his Spirit. Be filled with the Breath of God." We have to define our interpretation of what that should look like so people can skip the difficult step of relating to him and just go through the motions. We want to make sure people outwardly show what we hope is inwardly true.

Each religious tradition, including the Christian faith, has certain expectations about marriage, family life, work habits, worship styles, and much more—including prayer. Those of us in evangelical circles who learn about prayer through example and discipleship literature eventually develop methods of prayer, principles of prayer, keys to prayer, and so on. We can walk through any Christian bookstore and find numerous titles that offer to define prayer for us—and to conform us to the right image of prayer.

*The problem is that the conformity we teach sometimes doesn't reflect the image of Christ.*

The intentions behind discipleship aren't bad. After all, Scripture tells us to be "conformed" to the image of Christ. *Conformity* isn't a bad word. The problem is that the conformity we teach sometimes doesn't reflect the image of Christ as much as we think it does. Yes, we're to be conformed, but we're being conformed to the image of a Christ who broke traditions and defied expectations. We've put layers and layers of tradition on top of biblical practice, and the result often deprives God of the individual relationships he seeks. He doesn't get to enjoy the diversity he created us for.

I've often envisioned the Father scanning the landscape of earth in search of a billion personalities, only to find one group acting in one fashion, another group acting in another, and so on. Instead of a billion unique souls, he gets a handful of traditions—people trying to pray like so-and-so because so-and-so got a lot of answers and must have known the key to effective praying. And while God *does* in fact teach us consistent principles in the examples of Scripture and history, he never tells us what words to say or what posture to assume or what music to have in the background or what time of day is most spiritual or…well, you get the picture. We can exhaust ourselves thinking of the well-intentioned instructions we've received, when really all God wants is for us to communicate with him out of the hearts he gave us.

That's why we don't pray creatively; we impose limits on ourselves because we think that's what God wants. We become formula people, forgetting that he is not a formula God.

Some people have a formula that rules out emotional praying, others have one that rules out informal praying, and still others have one that rules out intimate praying. We stifle individuality for a false understanding of conformity to Christ.

Prayer may have some defining characteristics in Scripture— faith, honesty, and a kingdom agenda come to mind—but there are no biblical limits to the ways in which prayer is expressed. The Word is remarkably silent about the logistics and media of our expression. It has plenty to say about the content, but hardly anything about the delivery. The reason? If God wanted us to fit a mold, he would have made us from molds.


## STRANGE BREEDS

Some of our conformist excesses can be easily seen if we apply them to biblical characters. Let's take Abraham and Sarah, for example. Why weren't they content without a son? Didn't they know their identity and security were in God alone, not in being parents? That's the counsel we would have given them, and this ridiculous obsession with an absurd promise of God at their age would be a sign of serious spiritual immaturity, not faith. Yet the Bible's assessment of this couple is that their faith is the kind on which eternal kingdoms are built.

The same could be said of Hannah too. She also craved a child, and her reasons weren't entirely consistent with what we would consider "godliness."[23] She wanted to bear children partly because her rival, her husband's other wife, was cranking them out like a baby factory and taunting Hannah for her barrenness. We modern evangelicals would tell Hannah that envy is a poor motive for having kids and that the promise to offer a child to the priesthood is a transparent attempt to bribe and manipulate God. Yet Scripture affirms Hannah's desperate plea for motherhood, and her godly son kept God's chosen nation from spiraling downward into further corruption. Her "envy" and "manipulation," it seems, were valuable to God.

> *Hannah's "envy" and "manipulation," it seems, were valuable to God.*

Or consider David as another example. We quickly join with Scripture's condemnation of Michal, his wife, for her contempt of David as she watched him dance.[24] Seriously, though, if our president were seen in public dancing in front of a bunch of girls in his underwear and then saying it was all "for the Lord," wouldn't we be just a little embarrassed? Shouldn't *some* decorum go with the office? Can you imagine the editorials? The global shame? The impeachment?

Not only did biblical characters sometimes not conform to the religious standards of their cultures, they sometimes seemed even to stretch the boundaries set in place by God. If a man came to you and said that God told him to take his son up to a mountaintop and sacrifice him, what would you say? If another told you God had led him to marry a prostitute, how would you respond? If a young woman swore to you that she was pregnant but still a virgin, wouldn't you roll your eyes? Let's face it: modern evangelicalism would castigate all three of these people, as would their own cultures. Yet God himself was the One who led Abraham, Hosea, and Mary into those circumstances. If religious instincts would castigate them, they would also castigate God. In fact, when God clothed himself in flesh, that's exactly what those instincts did.

The truth is that biblical characters did some pretty strange things for often obscure and sometimes mixed motives, and we laud them for their faith and devotion. Retrospect allows us that privilege. But if the same characters—try Ezekiel, for a worst-case scenario—did some of those things today, our voices would join the chorus of judges. They would be embarrassing to us, and we could come up with lots of reasons that they just weren't behaving biblically or in a Christlike manner. And most of our embarrassment and judgment would be products not of the Holy Spirit's work in our hearts, but of the cultural expectations we have as Christians.

Our expectations when it comes to prayer usually aren't quite that extreme or stifling, but the evidence that we have them and apply them to all of Christian life is easy to see. We aren't purely biblical because we can't be. We were raised in a nonbiblical context, incorporating into our values and personalities the ethics and expectations of the age. There's no shame in that; we are unavoidably affected by the culture we live in. We just have to realize that and loosen up when it comes to assuming that our values are always biblical.

## Pharisees and Fads

We can't blame society for trying to conform us to its wishes. We try to conform ourselves. Young athletes spit and scratch like their favorite players. Young musicians conform to the nonconformity of rock icons. Men and women buy clothes, cut their hair, adopt the speech patterns, and embrace the values of Hollywood's most successful and intriguing stars. Boys grow up to be like Dad, and girls grow up to be like Mom.

Life is designed to work that way—to a degree. Jesus told his disciples that the servants would be like the master. Paul told the Corinthians to imitate him[25] and the Ephesians to imitate God.[26] And we are all being conformed to the image of Christ.[27] So *conformity* is not a bad word; we're made in God's image and being transformed back into the image of his Son. As a famous advertising slogan once said, "Image is everything." The trick is choosing the *right* image.

*Conformity is not a bad word.*

When most of us pray, we have an image in our mind of what prayer should look like. Some people envision the dark halls of a monastery. Others, the candles or kneeling cushions of a high, liturgical church. Still others imagine great missionaries like John Hyde or Hudson Taylor wrestling in intense intercession for hours at a time. But regardless of whether these images are valid—and usually they are—they often aren't good reflections of who we truly are, or they don't fit the circumstances in which we pray. We each have a specific picture, given to us by family tradition, church practice, or our own research, that may or may not express our own personality. And in order to fit that picture, we strip ourselves down and play a role. We seek the formula instead of the Father.

One situation in the Gospels where this dynamic showed up was when the religious authorities asked Jesus why his disciples didn't fast the way John the Baptist's disciples and the Pharisees did.[28] They weren't consciously trying to impose unbiblical standards on Jesus. In fact, they probably thought their assumptions were purely scriptural without any taint of cultural influence. But religious culture can be subtle, and in this case the implication was that the prayer life of Jesus' disciples wasn't godly or spiritual enough. They judged on the right evidence, but with false standards.

We do that, even with ourselves. We strive to fulfill some model of spirituality—monastic, mystical, contemplative, pietistic, whatever—not realizing that (1) it's a standard so high we're bound to fail, and (2) it's a standard that doesn't square fully with the revelation God has given us—or even with his own nature. The result is that we offer black-and-white pictures to a colorful God, or monotone words to a full-orchestra God. Our prayers don't seem to get us anywhere. We end up on a spiritual treadmill, always running but never progressing.

Don't believe it? Ask several of your friends if they are satisfied with their prayer lives, and see how many answer in the affirmative. My guess is that you won't get a single yes—I never have. Almost no one is satisfied with their prayer life because standards are impossibly high, methods are narrowly defined, and a heart-connection with God is usually absent. Something's wrong with that picture.

We can't blame God or Jesus or the Bible for the discrepancy between prayers and satisfaction. If we've gotten the wrong impression about prayer, it didn't come from the One who created us for the specific purpose of communing with him. It came instead from our own definitions, false expectations, and self-imposed limits. At the core of our dissatisfaction are some missing ingredients. I believe one of the biggest missing ingredients is the creative personality each of us has.

## CREATED BY A CREATOR

Let's go back to the artist filled with the Breath that hovers, whose name places him "under the shadow of God." He and his partner were summoned into the gap between God and man and were told to be creative. The mission to form gilded angels on the box of God, to provide the ornate details of the articles of worship, to weave the colors of divine royalty into the fabric of the holy tent, was given to Bezalel and Oholiab.

They aren't exactly household names, are they? They didn't part the Red Sea, slay Goliath, write psalms, prophesy to the nation, or any such work of spiritual power and leadership. No, they were artists. Craftsmen. Creative guys whose parents probably wanted them to get a real job. Moses had already gone into Egypt, pronounced plagues upon Pharaoh's kingdom, miraculously delivered his people through wilderness and water, and spoken face to face with God on a mountain, yet the first time the Holy Spirit actually inhabited someone was when God chose these men. Why? Because the Creator wanted his people to create something that would point to who he is.

*The Creator wanted his people to create something that would point to who he is.*

That's the way it should be. That tells us something about God. It doesn't tell us that he's an art lover regardless of the subject or purpose of the art. He isn't an enthusiast or collector of our random or self-inspired creations. He is, however, intensely interested in the sacred interaction between his people and himself. He loves the quiet, reflective times we spend with him, stilling our souls and waiting serenely in his presence. But that's not the apex of spirituality that we make it out to be. It's one color of an entire palette that includes prayers of conflict, wrestling matches with his will, co-crafting his mission strategies, charging with him into battle, and offering him the best we have. He has no problem with our tone reflecting zeal, hurt, anger, passion, or desire, or with any of the nonverbal forms of communication we use among friends and family. He loves to hear us not only singing *about* him but also *to* him, whether in church or in private. He wouldn't be embarrassed if we were to dance for him or draw him a picture.

Bezalel and Oholiab were blessed in their craft by the presence of God, but many after them have felt peripheral to the cause. Doesn't it seem odd that we believe we were made in the image of a *Creator*, and yet creativity is usually most freely expressed outside the church? If the Creator made us in his image, doesn't it stand to reason that we might best reflect who he is by being—dare I say it—*creative*?

Bezalel is no longer an exception. All believers have now been filled with the Breath that hovered and created. If it makes perfect sense to us that we are to be holy because he is holy, or that we are to be loving because he is love, why not that we are to be creative because he is creative, or expressive because he is expressive? Even during the Renaissance and Reformation eras, when the major patron of Europe's greatest artists was the church itself, artists' commissions were usually accompanied by a fairly precise and confining set of criteria. Rarely did an artist hear, "Paint whatever God inspires you to paint on the walls of our church!" They were given instructions. Great masters were able to craft beautiful works anyway, but there's no shortage of stories about patrons and clients butting heads over the creative process. There's always a tension between absolute truth and free expression. Both are given by God, but neither is very comfortable with the other.

This book isn't about art, but the subject is relevant because of how our faith has dealt with the creative process in the past. History tells us something about the relationship between religion and individuality, and it isn't always a happy story. Sometimes individuality really does conflict with Scripture and violate God's character—that's undeniable. But our spiritual attitudes toward creativity usually tend to err on the side of legalism rather than freedom. To stay on the safe side, we limit our styles and discourage nonconformists and misfits within the faith from venturing too far outside the culture.

We need to remind ourselves often that the current culture of our faith would also marginalize people like Ruth, Elijah, Elisha, Jeremiah, Ezekiel, Hosea, Esther, and many more. We would call them "misfits." If they had not already been approved in the pages of Scripture, we might not like them very much. They wouldn't fit our expectations—or our churches' expectations. That's because the church culture that looks so biblical to us would look so unbiblical to Christians of any other era, which in turn would look unbiblical to the first disciples. Culture is a strange stew, partly God's recipe and partly the added spices we're used to. But ours always tastes divine to us.

*Culture is a strange stew, partly God's recipe and partly the added spices we're used to. But ours always tastes divine to us.*

Sadly, that stew can taste very bitter to creative minds who feel as if they no longer belong among the people of God—not because of wrong theology or immoral behavior, but simply because prayer and praise come out of them differently.

Those of us who talk like the average Christian, walk like the average Christian, and worship like the average Christian enjoy the endorsement of the average church. We're "in." But those of us who play an instrument that doesn't blend with the worship band—literally or figuratively—or who dance for the Lord with unusual rhythm and movement—again, literally or figuratively—often feel that we need to strip ourselves of personality so we can be good disciples and grow in Christ.

The result? Godly people who never quite connect with the God who longs to connect with them.

## WHAT ARE YOU HIDING?

We've spent a lot of time on the individuality of human beings because it's pretty important to God. This chapter may come across like Barney telling preschoolers about how special they are, but it's more critical than that. The truth is that until you feel free to be you in your relationship with God, it's not a real relationship.

> *Until you feel free to be you*
> *in your relationship with God,*
> *it's not a real relationship.*

That's true on a human level—with spouse, friend, or anyone—so it shouldn't be hard for us to understand. But we forget that the nature of relationships with other people is a good reflection of the nature of a relationship with God. Just as we have to be real with those we love, we have to be real with God.

We can learn from great saints of today or bygone eras, but we can't just copy them and get the same results. What worked yesterday may not work today, and what didn't work yesterday may work today. God won't let us get locked into a principle because then we'd pursue principles instead of the Person. He related to the personalities of our faith heroes in their time and place, and the conditions have changed. We're not in the exact same situation, and we don't have the same personalities. Our relationship with him has to be somewhat different. And it can be as expressive and creative as we want it to be.

That raises a few questions for each of us: what aspect of your true personality do you suppress when you come to God? If it's something you know to be sinful, why not bring it to him and let him help you deal with it the way he promised? If it isn't sinful, why are you suppressing it? Is it because of pressure from family, peers, church, or the culture at large? Could it be something that God has uniquely placed in you in order to relate to him as no one else can?

## "WHEN I RUN..."

*Chariots of Fire* was a popular, Oscar-winning movie, so one of its most memorable quotes is by no means obscure. You've probably heard it in a sermon at least once or twice. It's the moment when the main character, Eric Liddell, is being urged by his sister to forsake the temporal treasures of Olympic running for the eternal treasures of the mission field. Her argument makes complete sense: competing to see which man is fastest has absolutely no eternal significance in the kingdom of God, whereas introducing people to Christ does.

Therefore, spending time on the mission field instead of wasting time on the track is a much wiser investment.

And Eric agrees, in principle. His heart *is* set on missions. But there is another side to his personality, a God-given gift that cries out to be used and enjoyed (as all God-given gifts do). His speed is an integral part of his relationship with God. So with much passion and purpose in his voice, he pleads his case: "When I run, I feel his pleasure. To give it up would be to hold him in contempt."

That's a good example of how Christian culture's most noble agenda can unwittingly suppress individual expression. God *did* use Eric Liddell on the mission field eventually, but first he used him to win an Olympic medal and become a living testimony for a generation of athletes. We even have a movie about him that still speaks volumes about being faithful to God in an unfaithful world.

*Creative, individual, personal communication with God expresses the nature of the kingdom like nothing else can.*

That's the power of creative, individual, personal communication with God. It expresses the nature of the kingdom like nothing else can. When we choose not to conform to expectations, God uses us beyond expectations. When we speak to him without formulas, he answers without formulas. And when we pray creatively, we delight our Creator.

# Three

# MORE THAN JUST WORDS

## The Mysterious Power of the Tongue

*W*ay back in the beginning, when the Spirit caressed the chaos and breathed his life into it, God's first recorded words dispelled the darkness. "Let there be light," he said, and there was light. No hesitation, no argument, no counterpoint from the darkness insisting on an explanation or a confirmation. God spoke, so it happened—just as he said.

We don't know what language God spoke. It certainly wasn't English, and it's pretty far-fetched to think it might have been one of the biblical languages of Hebrew or Greek. I have a hunch it was a language that had never been tried out on humans, since humans didn't exactly exist yet. So what was it? Did the angels understand it, or was it God's private tongue? Was it even an audible voice? After all, sound waves were part of a physical world still in the early stages of construction. "Audible" doesn't mean a whole lot when the laws of physics haven't been implemented yet.

God's native language is an unfathomable mystery to us. But in spite of all that we don't know, we can be pretty sure his voice isn't one-dimensional. Given his penchant for speaking in pictures, there's a good chance his first language is visional, or perhaps involving senses we've never even heard of. Regardless, we do know this: it's alive, and it's powerful.

Before we dismiss words as a flat, uncreative medium for prayer—which portions of this book will appear to do—perhaps we should explore how powerful they can be when backed by God. The truth is that our words are insufficient expressions not simply because they're words; more accurately, it is because of how unimaginatively we sometimes use them. Just because we can all vaguely remember times of corporate or personal prayer that sounded like we were reading the phone book doesn't mean that's the only way to pray audibly. We who are made in the image of God ought to be able to speak words that are alive and powerful too.

> *We who are made in the image of God ought to be able to speak words that are alive and powerful.*

From the creation story we get the impression that God didn't just speak words; he spoke *authority.* That's often what words in the Bible really are: powerful, creative expressions. There's a huge difference between voices that offer up suggestions, descriptions, pleas, or ideas, and voices that articulate concrete reality.

We are told in Scripture that God "calls things that are not as though they were."[29] God spoke light before there was light, so there was light. Words and the act of creation were inseparable.

## CREATIVE LANGUAGE

There's biblical evidence that this is our pattern for faith. It isn't an exact pattern, as God is the only One who can create something out of nothing. But the context in which Paul tells us that God "calls things that are not as though they [are]" is a discussion of Abraham's faith. "Against all hope, Abraham in hope believed."[30] He embraced this word about invisible things and agreed with it. He and Sarah surely talked about it, and not in a way that would undermine their faith. They spoke words that were in line with God's will and authority, and amazing things happened. Why? Because words are powerful.

This is why Isaac spoke a blessing over Jacob, thinking Jacob was Esau, and couldn't just "take it back" after it was spoken.[31] It's also why Balaam couldn't just speak the curse over Israel that Balak wanted him to speak and trust that it would have no effect. He tried, but he was compelled to utter the truth of God's intentions.[32] The text implies that a curse would have been effectual; therefore God didn't permit it. Scripture clearly affirms that words are concrete: they have the power of life and death,[33] they set the course of a life on fire,[34] and people will be accountable to God for every careless word they utter.[35] We are strongly urged in the Bible to bless and not curse,[36] to put aside perverse and corrupt speech,[37] to remember that what comes out of our mouths can make us unclean,[38] and to speak as though we were uttering the very words of God.[39]

The Word strongly emphasizes the importance of using words appropriately. They are central to life. We're even told that "in the beginning was the Word, and the Word was with God, and the Word was God."[40] The connection between language and the creative power of God (and those made in his image) is mysterious but certain.

But we take words casually. After all, aren't they a plentiful commodity? They don't cost anything to use, and throwing them around can be fun. We've all said things that don't come to pass and seen things come true that weren't spoken, so we know words aren't always concrete and effectual. We coin expressions like "You're all talk and no action" and "Don't worry about what he said; it's just words." And then there's the classic: "Sticks and stones will break my bones, but words will never hurt me." Yeah, right. Words mean nothing— or so we keep telling ourselves, hoping we'll be convinced.

We never get that impression from Scripture, though. And truth be told, experience teaches us about the power of words just as often as it teaches us about their impotence. They can wound the soul, sometimes mortally. They can set nation against nation and brother against brother. They carry the awesome privilege of blessing the Father and the shameful disgrace of cursing our neighbor. Each of us has, at one time or another, discovered the inviolable principle that once something is said, it can't be unsaid. And the regret that follows can plague us for years.

But the Bible takes the importance of the spoken word even further than being simply an emotional or psychological weapon for good or evil—though there's certainly a lot of power in that weapon. Prophecies, blessings, and curses, in particular, seem to be weighty and substantial. They are intended to have an effect, much more so than the words of a normal conversation. They affirm the stated intentions of the heart—and, when flowing out of a relationship with God, the stated intentions of *his* heart. Not only do they express reality, they influence it.

Occultists seem to know this, which is why many "strange but true" experiences and stories have convinced people that incantations and curses are real. We know that they can't usurp the authority of

Christ or harm someone whose life is in him, but we can't say that they always fall to the ground harmlessly. The revelation God has given us insists that angels and demons are present and listening and that they can be stirred to action by and on behalf of human beings. Angels are ministering spirits, we are told,[41] God's spiritual messengers who minister for good. We can assume from Scripture's witness that ungodly spirits minister for evil. Often, that sort of ministry is prompted by human speech.[42]

This idea bothers many people. Though it fits into biblical culture, it doesn't fit ours very well. It sounds too superstitious for rational people like us. But nowhere does Scripture indicate that Satan's counterfeits are very far removed from God's truths. In fact, any effective counterfeit will closely resemble the real thing. Occult practices take what is right and good, and they distort and defile it; they mock the truth by mimicking and caricaturing it. They co-opt God's principles and use them for an evil agenda. And while God certainly never tells us to go around pronouncing spells and curses, he does tell us to use our mouths to speak words of faith and to bless people. Why? Because words have real power in real life.[43]

## WATER AND THE WORD

Japanese scientist Masaru Emoto has conducted extensive research on the effects of words on water. In many of his experiments, he has obtained pure spring water from a single source, put it in test tubes, and then exposed each test tube to either positive or negative words. Water samples exposed to expressions like "thank you," "I love you," and "peace" are separated from samples exposed to expressions like "you're worthless," "I hate you," and "war." When the samples placed in an environment of positive words are then frozen, their microscopic crystals show beautiful, intricate patterns and shapes. When frozen samples from the negative environment are examined, their crystals are sludgy and shapeless.

That in itself is fascinating, but when the experiments are carried even further with written words instead of audible words—phrases are written on slips of paper and taped to the side of the test tube—the results are the same. A schoolkid in Japan learned of Dr. Emoto's research and decided to try the theory out on leftover rice. After a couple of weeks in the refrigerator, rice in a container with positive words written on the side remained white and relatively odor-free. Its unfortunate counterpart, with some discouraging verbiage written on it, turned brown and smelly. The only difference—at least in the highly controlled experiments of Emoto, if not with the rice in the fridge—was the verbal environment in which samples were placed. Simple words were powerful. As Emoto says, "Beautiful words create beautiful nature. Ugly words create ugly nature."[44]

Emoto does not claim a biblical worldview, so he draws conclusions that don't necessarily reflect Christian beliefs. This principle of words' effects can easily be adopted by New Age devotees, atheistic evolutionists, Buddhist or Hindu mystics, or anyone else who wants to hijack it for their own purposes. But that shouldn't nullify the results of his experiments, which explore a principle in God's creation. In light of the Bible's emphasis on the power of language—from the "let there be light" of God to the "bless and curse not" of people—it isn't hard to find Christian principles in his research, is it? God has written into creation a cause-and-effect dynamic with the spoken word.

That thought is awfully sobering, considering the verbal abuse that goes on between spouses, between parents and children, and in many other kinds of relationships. Water is a somewhat neutral casualty of negative words; with children, for example, the stakes are astronomically higher. We know that criticism and threats can have powerful emotional effects, and that emotions in turn have physiological effects. But Emoto's research indicates a direct correlation between words and physical well-being. That alone should cause us to think twice about what we say.

Though the thought is sobering, it certainly makes sense. From the voice that commanded order in the tumultuous waters of the deep, to the voice from the throne that says, "Behold, I am making all things new,"[45] the spoken word is powerful. No wonder Jesus said people would be accountable for every careless word they speak.[46]

> *No wonder Jesus said people would be accountable for every careless word they speak.*

What does this mean for prayer? If we're talking about the casual conversation kind of prayer we usually engage in, probably not much. There's nothing wrong with that kind of prayer, though it does seem to undermine the priority of our requests sometimes. But when we are aware that our words carry impact and we see them as formal petitions—or when directed outward to people and circumstances rather than upward to God—we begin to measure them carefully and expect consequences. They aren't hit-and-miss buckshot; they're sharply aimed arrows, and we ought to be surprised if they don't hit a target.

When we understand the power of words, our conversations change. That includes our conversations with God.

If we were summoned to the Oval Office to present our agenda for the country, would we spend any time to prepare? To measure our words carefully to make sure they were appropriate? To express them in the most memorable way possible, so they'd linger in the mind of the chief executive? Of course we would.

Yet we often come into the throne room of God with a hospital registry or our daily to-do list, or with a tone near apologizing for even hoping for a response. We're like a congressional aide spelling out all the boring details of a routine bill, having no real understanding of whether its passage is likely or even feasible. Surely God meant for our words to mean more than that—especially in the context of a familiar, intimate relationship with him. We forget that words are meaningful, purposeful, and very powerful.

## AMAZING WORDS

People were amazed at the authority of Jesus' words.[47] On one occasion, he told a storm to calm down—and it did.[48] On another occasion, he told a fig tree to dry up and die—and it did.[49] When he commanded that a multitude be miraculously fed, it was. When he told people to be healed, they were. When he shouted, "Lazarus, come forth!" a dead guy got up and walked.[50] When he said, "I am he," his opponents fell to the ground.[51] When Jesus spoke, stuff happened.

*When Jesus spoke, stuff happened.*

"But that's Jesus," we counter. "He's the Son of God!" Yes, but we are his adopted brothers and sisters. Toward the end of the Gospel of John, the disciples were gathered in a locked room. Jesus showed up—you can do that when you know your voice is more authoritative than the lock on the door—and gave his disciples an amazing mission: "As the Father has sent Me, I also send you." The same message, the same sacrifice, the same power, the same authority. And then he got in their faces, and the God who had breathed into Adam's face millennia before, who had breathed into two craftsmen of holy articles, now breathed his Holy Breath into these men who had followed him.[52] He hovered and brooded and imparted new life. And that Spirit, not long afterward, breathed into multitudes of believers. He still does. Same creative power, same purpose, same message. As the Father sent him, that's how he sends us.

So why don't we see the same results from our spoken words that Jesus saw from his? That's the question that ought to plague every believer until the answer is "We do." I've seen people who believe in the power of the spoken word speak miracles into existence. It happens. According to Scripture, there's no reason it shouldn't.[53] Words are alive.

On one occasion when Jesus taught his disciples about faith and prayer, he said, "Truly I say to you, whoever says to this mountain, 'Be taken up and cast into the sea,' and does not doubt in his heart, but believes that what he says is going to happen, it will be granted him."[54] For some reason, he didn't say that whoever prayed about the mountain would see it move. The prayer involved speaking to the mountain itself. The implication is that the word of a person of faith can be directed to the mountain—under God's authority, of course—and the command will carry power.

That's why he's able to tell his disciples to heal people and raise the dead.[55] We'd expect him to say, "Pray for people to be healed." But no, he doesn't give us the privilege of deferring all things to him, even though both he and we know he's the source of all power. He tells us to heal in his name, just as he told the disciples to feed a multitude, just as he told them they could wither a fig tree the same way he did. There's no hint in Jesus' ministry that his followers would be left without the creative power of the spoken word, either in prayer or in direct confrontation against evil. Our words, like his, can breathe the Breath of life into dust.

So why don't they? Maybe it's because we just don't believe. Maybe it's because we start out believing and then our doubts nag us into throwing in the towel and saying, "Well, Jesus is Jesus and we're not," even though he clearly endowed us with his Spirit—the Spirit who hovered and breathed life into chaos. Maybe it's because we've invented a theology of impotence that defines the dynamic of God being strong in our weakness as some obscure, imperceptible phenomenon. Or maybe we've just decided the promises of Scripture are too good to be true.

Whatever the case, the spoken word has proven amazingly powerful for certain people in certain ages and certain situations. People *have* been healed. Some have even been raised from the dead.[56] Peter and John told a paralytic to get up and walk, and their words bore obvious fruit.[57] Paul boldly called blindness down on a sorcerer, and his words didn't prove impotent.[58] Both in their relationship with God and with others, New Testament believers declared the creativity of the kingdom and saw it spring up. They spoke into a spiritual chaos, and the chaos obeyed.

That doesn't mean that we can just say whatever we want and it will happen—the "name it and claim it" approach so roundly criticized in Christendom. But our reactions against elements of that movement have often gone to the opposite extreme and thus denied any effective power of verbal expression. And the evidence from many Christ-honoring, faithful churches and believers, both in the Bible and in subsequent history, is that the spoken word in the name of Jesus can accomplish miracles.

There are times, of course, when there's nothing. No healing, no resurrection, no answers. The spoken word can be surprisingly potent on some occasions and disappointingly impotent on others. What's the difference? I don't know, and I don't have to. Scripture doesn't give us a black-and-white explanation. But for anyone with eyes of faith, the disappointments don't nullify the miracles. I can't explain why the cause and effect of faith and words and prayer isn't easy to understand. All I know is that sometimes a spoken word in the name of Jesus turns death into life.

## BREATH INTO DUST, REVISITED

Ezekiel looked out into the valley before him. Bones everywhere. Dry bones. Dusty remains of thousands who had died. And the God who spread out this valley in Ezekiel's vision didn't just roll the tape and let the prophet see the plan. Ezekiel had a substantial part to play. "Prophesy over these bones," God told him.

> Say to them, "O dry bones, hear the word of the LORD."
> Thus says the Lord GOD to these bones, "Behold, I will cause breath to enter you that you may come to life."

So Ezekiel spoke, and the dusty bones joined together and grew flesh. Still, there was no life in them. Like Adam long before, thousands of creatures of dust lay lifeless on the ground, waiting for the Breath of God.

> "Prophesy to the breath," said the Lord. "Say to the breath, 'Thus says the Lord GOD, "Come from the four winds, O breath, and breathe on these slain, that they come to life."'"

So Ezekiel spoke again, this time to the breath—yes, *that* Breath—and the bones obeyed. The Spirit who hovers and exhales did his work again, and order came out of chaos, life came out of death. Hints of Genesis blew in with the breeze.[59]

Why did God need a prophet? He was going to restore Israel anyway. Why this picture of dry bones coming to life and forming a great army? Why have Ezekiel speak to the bones, as if God's voice wasn't the only one needed? And why in two stages, as if the first word from the Lord wasn't quite enough to get the job done?

These are mysteries, and we don't have to answer them. We have the privilege of being silent where God is silent. But we don't have the privilege of discounting the prophet's role and minimizing the importance of the human voice echoing the divine voice according to God's will. What God declares, we can declare. In fact, that's often exactly what we're called to do.

### TRAINED AND TRUSTED

The Air Force F-22 Raptor is the most expensive fighter jet built to date. It's a supersonic stealth fighter virtually invisible to radar and infrared sensors, and it can track enemy aircraft and targets without its location being detected. It's a high-tech, precision piece of machinery, and it's armed to the hilt. And it costs over $130 million per plane.

Flying an F-22 Raptor requires extensive training and a keen ability to make quick, life-or-death decisions. It takes a superior sense of confidence and an uncommon level of intelligence. Slight mishandling could result in loss of life—and of a significant portion of the military budget. No rival of the U.S. has one at this point, and from an American perspective, it's best that way. In the wrong hands, an armed Raptor could do quite a bit of damage. It could be devastating.

Can you imagine turning such powerful, sensitive, and expensive equipment over to someone in his early twenties? Well, you don't have to imagine it. The Air Force does it all the time. Young men and women who, only a few years earlier, could not be trusted with Mom and Dad's car keys are suddenly given license to pilot the world's most advanced fighter. Only those with demonstrated maturity and a history of stability could even hope to qualify, and no one argues otherwise. It makes sense that this awesome power should be entrusted only to those who are trustworthy.

That's a pretty accurate picture of the power of words available to human beings—especially words of prayer. We don't realize what we're flying. There's plenty of evidence of our ignorance, the casualties of words strewn across the landscape of our lives. Critical people wound others. People who talk about being sick all the time are frequently sick all the time. People who talk about being victimized all the time are somehow victimized all the time. Conversely, people who talk about being blessed all the time seem to be blessed all the time.

Arguments about cause and effect—whether the talk causes the condition or vice versa—are off base by pinning responsibility on one or the other. It's a mutually debilitating (or beneficial) relationship: conditions beget attitudes, which beget talk, which can either feed or starve the original conditions. The fact is that people in the midst of difficulties frequently either talk themselves into further adversity or talk their way out of it. The cycle fuels itself until it's broken. While this isn't an invariable dynamic—because, as we know,

God isn't a formulaic God—it's true more often than not. And the reason we don't usually recognize the dynamic is because we don't understand the "jet" that's been turned over to us.

If all this speculation about the awesome power of words turned out to be true, would you continue using them conventionally, offering weightless prayers that you hardly remember the next week? Or would you measure them carefully and then launch them precisely, realizing that they will have an effect wherever they land? And if words carry such power, can you imagine the potential of using them more creatively? More descriptively? More emotionally...and imaginatively?

> *If words carry such power,*
> *can you imagine the potential*
> *of using them more creatively?*

Sometimes your life seems formless and void, dark and deep, a tumult of primeval waters drowning any sense of order and beauty. You need to know that a Voice hovers over your sea and a Creator leans over you to breathe his Spirit into your world. But this isn't a unilateral creation; you've already been made and remade in the image of God, and you have a voice too. Your conversations with the Spirit who hovers over you are powerful and purposeful to call new creation forth—together. Your heart-to-heart talks establish the kingdom of God, which stirs your Savior to action. The Breath fills your soul. His words and yours collaborate to restore what was lost and to birth what is new. The intimacy of dialogue is no casual matter; it moves the Maker of a vast universe.

Your prayers can be like God's voice piercing the darkness of original chaos, or like Jesus' shout calling Lazarus from the tomb. As a voice in a dark world, you can speak words of light and life, and those words will mean something. They're concrete. They can blow God's breath into dead piles of dust and cause a kingdom garden to spring up in place of a devastated, fallen landscape. They're words, but they're not the kind of words most of us usually pray. Yes, we can pray more creatively than spoken language will allow, and probably more powerfully too. We'll explore those possibilities in the following chapters. But even in the arena of verbal expression, we can get a lot more creative than we currently are.

God welcomes that. A lot of people don't know how open he is to our breaking form and letting loose with the raw power of the tools he's given us. Though he doesn't usually operate by formulas, we do. But in Scripture, he urges us through example and instruction to get beyond formulas in our relationship with him. We have few instances, if any, of Jesus' responding to an expected, canned approach, but many instances of his honoring unconventional seekers.[60] If he honors lack of convention in the actions of those who came to him, he certainly doesn't refuse it in the words of those who speak to him.

> The Voice that long ago said, "Let there be light," has offered us the power of blessing others and praising him.

When you use words to pray, use them creatively. Use them well. Be as descriptive as you want to be and as purposeful as words will allow. The Voice that long ago said, "Let there be light," has offered us the power of blessing others and praising him, of speaking words of faith before sight gives us permission, of declaring light in places of darkness, and of claiming truth in places of deception. That's an amazingly powerful tool in your calling to shape your world. Become a master artisan in your ability to use it.

*Four*

## Praying like a Charapa

The people of the Amazon region of northern Peru are called Charapas. They are known and loved in the rest of the country for their unique cultural distinctives, one of which is their expressiveness. When a Charapa tells a story, he can't sit still and he doesn't just use words. He uses sound effects, imitates the expressions of the characters, mimics the movements of any animals in the story, acts out the plot, and even includes his listeners as props. It's as close to a multimedia presentation as a human being unacquainted with high-tech gadgets can offer.

The richness of that kind of expression is appealing to most people. Each of us has, at one time or another, checked out mentally during an oral presentation. The reason is that unless we're already highly motivated to absorb the content of the presentation, the drone of a long-winded speaker holds little interest for us. It engages only one of our senses, and for most of us, having only one sense operating is like dangling over boredom by a thread. It's pretty easy to fall.

Good communicators know that engaging more than just the ears of the audience enhances the audience's attention span and memory. According to research, we retain approximately 10 percent of what we read, 20 percent of what we hear, 30 percent of what we see, 50 percent of what we see *and* hear, 70 percent of what we say and write, and 90 percent of what we do.[61] The more senses are involved, the more effective the communication.

> *The more senses are involved,*
> *the more effective the communication.*

When we pray, we don't really need to worry about God's attention span or his ability to remember what we've said. Obviously, the omniscient Creator who made us sees into our hearts and has no memory lapses. But our prayers don't develop the relationship if we're so bored we can't remember them ourselves. Half the time when God answers us, we don't recognize the answer because the context of the relationship has progressed and we don't recall what we asked.

If we want to feel fully connected in our communication with our God, prayer can't be like a boardroom presentation. It has to be richer, fuller, and warmer than that. It has to be alive and active, deep and true, passionate and persistent. It has to have personality.

In a way, we need to pray Charapa prayers. They don't need to include all the sound effects and motions—although that would be fun and entertaining, both for ourselves and for God—but they do need to have us and our Listener fully engaged. As much as possible, they need to incorporate all of our personality, all of our gifts and talents, and all of our imagination. They should sometimes involve movement, music, mental pictures, physical objects, parables, favorite lyrics, prophetic actions, and any other sights, smells, and tastes we can think of.

Exactly *how* we accomplish this is an individual matter, but the point is that limiting our prayers to the equivalent of a recorded voice message is completely unnecessary and usually unsatisfying. There's no reason to detach from ourselves or our surroundings in order to say the right things to God.

## A GARDEN WITHOUT MASKS

I have a confession to make: I watch Spanish soap operas.

I love studying languages, and the *telenovelas* on Spanish cable stations make it interesting. You can pick up a lot of phrases and train your ear to hear a foreign language's cadence and syntax when you listen to it in the context of a story. In fact, I'd watch anything with a plot in almost any language. It's a great way to learn.

On a good day of *telenovela* viewing, I understand what I'm hearing pretty well. Sometimes, however, I hardly understand a word. One evening recently, I was in one of those confused moments and getting pretty frustrated about it. A lot of plot development was happening, and I was missing it because my ears couldn't keep up. A woman with fiery red hair and a matching personality was running her mouth at about five thousand words per minute. She was speaking, of course, to a man who just didn't get it. Apparently, she was a jilted lover.

*I'm pretty sure,* I thought, *that the old playwright who wrote that line about hell having no fury like a woman scorned had just watched a Latina on a soap opera.* I saw nostrils flaring, tears forming, saliva

spraying, skin reddening, and laserlike eyes that could have pene-
trated any bank vault on the planet. I felt a strange urge to go throw
a football with the guys until the scene was over. I was genuinely
thankful not to be the dope who'd rejected her.

Then I realized that without understanding a word, I pretty
much knew what was going on in that scene. The woman with hell's
fury said that she had been treated unfairly, that she had given her
man everything he needed and it still wasn't enough, that he was a
lying, hypocritical, stupid, insensitive fool, that her child was suffer-
ing the consequences of his misbehavior, and that he had irrevoca-
bly broken the relationship and she was therefore moving out. And
she said all that through nonverbal expression.

We can say a lot without actually saying a lot. Not only do we
use words, we combine them with a variety of facial expressions, gestures, and tones. Sometimes we yell and shout, and sometimes we
whisper. We create artistic devices like drama, music, and visual arts
to express universal themes and nuances of the human soul. Our
clothes and hairstyles tell people something about our personality.
We shed tears, smile, and send messages with our body language. We
affectionately touch people we love, and sometimes that affection
leads to depths of intimacy. Most of us have little problem expressing ourselves—to people.

*We can say a lot
without actually saying a lot.*

We behave differently with God. Sometimes a prayer is just a
thought, and we know he understands us. Though we forget 90
percent of the previous day's relationship that way, it's still valid

communication. But even inwardly, we wear a lot of masks when we use our words, when we form our thoughts into mental sentences. We position ourselves as pure when we know we aren't, or we play the victim when we've victimized ourselves or others, or we tell God one motive when deep down we have another. Our hidden thoughts are often hidden even to us, and our expression in prayer reflects our ignorance.

God, however, knows all the nuances of our soul. He wants honesty in our prayers—not so he can find out what's really going on, but so he can relate to us on the basis of what's really going on.

Creative expression in our prayers—for example, gestures, sounds, countenance, posture, objects, and music—is a way of taking the masks off and having a full and rich relationship with our Creator. When we let loose with what's in us, we find God actually responding to what's in us. And the best way to let loose is to bring every feeling and all five senses into the conversation.

That's how it was in Eden, I'm sure. There were no masks, at least not at first—not until that day Adam and Eve felt compelled to hide in the bushes (in the Wind of the evening, no less) because they disobeyed the One who had breathed his creative Breath into them. They tried to escape the gaze of the hovering Spirit who spoke life and beauty into the lifeless dust and deep. But until that wretched experience, there was open communion between the Creator and the created, and masks were completely unnecessary.

Redemption was designed to restore the communion of Eden to us—actually, to restore it and improve on it. God made a very tangible Garden in which to enjoy fellowship with those made in his image, and after the Fall, he specified tangible forms of communication to express that fellowship. Every time the Bible mentions a burnt sacrifice, the aroma of incense, the symbols of Israel's festivals, or the bread and the wine, it refers to some kind of concrete, non-verbal evidence of whatever's in the heart of the communicator. If God had been content just to know what's in our hearts, he wouldn't have given us so many instructions about making our faith, obedience, and prayers visible. Certainly he knows our inward thoughts, but he takes great pleasure in the outward expression of them.

Look at it this way: If you could read the mind of your husband or wife and perceive every thought and emotion contained in it, would you be content never to hear his or her voice? Never to hold hands? Never to enjoy a fine meal in a candlelit room? Never to see your wife in a gorgeous dress, or your husband in a fine suit? Never to receive an anniversary gift? Never to feel the warm breath of intimacy on your face?

Perhaps this is why Hebrew words used in the Bible for praise and worship almost always have some connotation of movement or sound. In our Bibles, we read "praise" for all of them and think of words. In the original text, one word implies singing, another means "to extend one's hands," another means "to bow," another describes the act of playing an instrument, another implies a clamorous celebration, and others refer to dancing or shouting. Each refers to a different expression—an outward representation of an inner thought.

Yes, God knows our thoughts. We don't have to tell him how we feel or what we want. But how could he *not* enjoy it when we do? He made us with five senses; he receives pleasure when we use them to express our love and gratitude to him.

*God receives pleasure when we use*
*our five senses to express*
*our love and gratitude to him.*

## SOMETHING TO SHOW FOR IT

I remember when my son Timothy said to me, "I made this for you"—and there in his chubby little hand was a colorful drawing of a jet-propelled race car (because, he said, the regular stock cars on television just don't get around the track fast enough). I was touched. How could I not be moved by such a gesture? Timothy suggested that I take the picture with me to work and put it on my desk, where I could see it and think of him throughout the day. Plus, he added, it would be a helpful reminder of a good gift idea for his birthday, which was only seven months away.

Timothy is always making things like that for me. He's a little older now, so he understands that jet engines aren't really well suited for stock cars. But that hasn't hindered his designs for new vehicles; I've seen plenty of concept cars that I'm sure will be on the road one day, if BMW or Hummer gives them a look. I've also seen an amargasaur injure a larger but unsuspecting iguanodon with its whiplike tail—and the iguanodon's mother gently tending to her baby's wounds. All manner of dinosaurs, vehicles, Lego creations, and much, much more have been given to me as gifts of affection. I love them. They express the heart of my child and provide visible subjects around which we can bond.

One busy week a few years ago, one of my sons petitioned me several times to play soccer with him. I kept saying, "Yeah, that would be fun. We need to do that soon. But not today—I've got too much to do." A few days later, he brought me a picture he'd drawn with crayons. It was him and me in the yard, holding hands, and a soccer ball between us. I got the hint. That picture moved me more powerfully than any of his verbal requests earlier in the week had done. Words told me what he wanted to do. His drawing revealed his heart's desire. We were out in the yard almost immediately because he had shown me the connection he was craving.

King David had an "I made this for you" kind of heart. He wanted to go get the ark of the covenant and bring it to Jerusalem—and, after a rough start, he did. He desperately wanted to build God a temple, and although God appreciated the gesture, he deferred the privilege to David's son Solomon. David's psalms reflect a desire to honor God and express his heart to the One he loved.

History is full of extravagant gifts like that—of artists who color the canvas with raw emotion as an act of devotion to their beloveds, or of musicians who write ballads because words alone aren't enough to express how they feel. One of the world's most famous expressions of love is the Taj Mahal, a monument to an Indian queen who died in childbirth at the age of thirty-nine. Her husband, the king, was inconsolable at her death, and for two years in the royal court, there was no music, no celebration, no feasting—in other words, no creativity. Eventually he decided to build a monument so the world would remember the woman he loved. A garden by a river was selected as the site; the country's most skilled architects, masons, and calligraphers were commissioned; expensive materials were imported from far and wide; and some twenty years of meticulous craftsmanship later, a landmark was finished. Without the Taj, Mumtaz Mahal would be a footnote buried under five centuries of oblivion. Instead, she is the main character of a well-known love story—all because the man who loved her poured his love into a tangible expression.

Jesus himself blessed tangible expressions of love. One night at dinner, a woman came to him with a flask of expensive ointment, broke it, poured it over his head, and wiped his feet with her hair.

The disciples, particularly Judas, thought she was being wasteful—too extravagant, too outside-the-box, too undignified. If she wanted to tell him "thanks" or "I love you," she could have just said so. Words would have communicated the message, wouldn't they? And surely the Son of God already knew how she felt, just as he once peeked into the heart of a woman at a well. A costly alabaster container filled with precious oil and spices could have been spared.

But Jesus endorsed her behavior. It was a creative expression of what was in her heart, a memorial to someone still alive, a tangible sacrifice from a very real love. And Jesus said it would be a *lasting* memorial. "Wherever the gospel is preached throughout the world, what she has done will also be told, in memory of her."[62] Her love, unspoken, would become part of the unchanging Word of God forever.

## LET IT OUT

Love has to express itself. Anyone who has loved understands how hard it is, how excruciatingly painful it is, to keep quiet about it or pretend it doesn't exist. Our deepest emotions can remain deep for only so long before they start to hurt us. The human heart yearns to reveal itself, just as God revealed his heart when his hands formed a human shape and his Breath blew into that dusty earthen vessel. All creation, at least in its original beauty, is a visible monument to the passions of the Creator. And as those who are made in his image, our passions will likewise find ways to express themselves creatively.

If not, those passions turn inward and make us feel as if we're going to die. Unexpressed love is like a stallion in a stable. If it stays confined too long, it goes stir-crazy and starts damaging things. Love bursts out from where it's sheltered—all intense emotions do. With monumental effort, the wild horses of the soul can somehow be subdued for a time, but they can't be muzzled forever.

*Love bursts out from where it's sheltered—all intense emotions do.*

This is why art therapy is often an effective treatment for people with emotional problems. Something unresolved within a scarred, sealed-up soul will damage and paralyze that soul until it can be rooted out. Expression is part of the process.

There's a balance, of course. No one wants to be around those who always wear their emotions on their sleeves and have no filters on their mouths because they just have to be "who they are." Sometimes the expression of anger and bitterness fuels the anger and bitterness; such feelings often need to be confessed rather than expressed. Not every fleeting emotional impulse needs to be aired. But the deep and lasting ones do, at least discreetly, and with someone trustworthy. We have to own up—with ourselves and with God—to the passions deep within.

We can see throughout the history of human creativity how passions crave expression. Take a look at today's music, for example. Some of it is intended as a cute commentary on trivial themes, but in most cases you'll find all sorts of intense feelings. Some love-struck guy is all hyped up over some girl—that's the basis for the vast majority of popular songs ever written—or some girl is hopelessly in love with the man of her dreams. Or, on the other side of the coin, the guy is completely torn apart by how she has broken his heart, or she's devastated by how carelessly he has treated her.

Songs explore other emotional themes as well. The music of the streets has rough edges of bitterness and anger. The alternative scene oozes with the angst and ennui of hopelessness. You can hear the broken lives, the poverty, the violence, and any other cry of the society's marginalized in the rhythms coming from your radio. Emotions bleed in many colors, from gangsta to goth and beyond. All because the things we deeply feel are relentless in their desire to be released.

## Make It Real

This impulse for expression is put within us by the One who made us—who expressed himself by making us in his image. Through ignorance of sacred things, the human race has turned our expression and our love to lesser matters. We have a divine impulse, which, in its fallen state, knows nothing of the divine; but it *must* be satisfied through expression, so we direct it toward whatever holds the most meaning for us at the moment.

This is why contemporary love songs often have a life-consuming, ultimate-meaning, all-or-nothing passion in them. Romantic love is our age's object of worship, just as it has been in ages past.

When God is marginalized from our public arena and from our own internal consciousness, romantic love is really the best thing remaining. We worship it by default. It comes closer to satisfying the soul and the senses than any other earthly gift, so that's what we sing about, make movies about, and write novels about. In most of the art we create, the subject involves either love gone right or love gone wrong. When we breathe out our feelings, they come out in an intense desire for personal connection.

Think that's an overstatement? Consider our culture's pop worship hymnal, which includes such lyrics as:

- "How am I supposed to live without you?"[63]
- "I'd walk a thousand miles if I could just see you."[64]
- "Take me as I am—take my life; I would give it all."[65]
- "I can't live, if living is without you."[66]
- "You're everything I know that makes me believe, I'm not alone."[67]
- "If you told me to die for you, I would."[68]
- "If I ever lose my faith in you, there'd be nothing left for me to do."[69]

These are not statements directed to God; they are directed to other human beings. Significant others. Lovers. Soul mates. Yet they have deeply religious cravings in them. They are spiritual impulses redirected by human passions. They reach for God and find only people.

Our culture is just screaming for someone to love with all its heart. The desperate impulse within our souls that tells us we must have an all-consuming passion is a legitimate impulse. We must believe in something deeply enough that it's more important than life itself. As much as we try to categorize this impulse as pathological, it isn't. We were made for it. We've just pointed it in the wrong direction.

One song made popular a few years ago is, like most other songs ever written, about a guy who has it bad for a girl. There's an all-or-nothing feel about it: the girl is the guy's reason for living. One memorable line goes, "Gimme your heart, make it real, or else forget about it."[70]

That would be good theology, if it were intended as such. Isn't that essentially the message God delivers to Israel through Isaiah,

Jeremiah, Ezekiel, and others? Isn't that what Jesus says to the Pharisees? To his disciples? To us?

The message of the song is that true love is not superficial. It's real. Going through the motions isn't enough. Sincere, heartfelt expression is what it's all about. Even a pagan world seems to know that. There's a lot of divine truth like this in our secular culture.

We have an abundance of unintentional prophets. Sacred realities are shouted from our radios and video screens, only no one seems to know who they should be directed toward. Even in our natural impulses, we seem to know a thing or two about love and how to express it.

As Christians in a secular society, we in some ways occupy a privileged position. We have been immersed in a creative culture—which the church often frowns on for its content—and we actually know the One who is ultimately worthy of our love. We've got both pieces of the puzzle, the creativity and the purpose, and yet many of us still aren't sure how to put them together. Our innovative culture has long told us that artistic expression is for real life, not a life of faith, and our faith culture has told us that artistic expression is usually corrupt and not a priority of the gospel anyway.

That's changing, as Western evangelicalism is going through some semblance of a renaissance. But we've only just started. Somehow we've got to put the puzzle together. We've got to embody the underlying message of the song. We've got to make it real.

How do we make it real? God knows how authentic our love for him is, whether we express it or not…but we don't know. Neither do the people around us. And even though God knows for his own sake, he gave us a Bible full of ways to make love manifest. Scripture's pages are covered with examples of what it means to love God outwardly. Our relationship with him has never been simply about inward thoughts and emotions. It shows up in what we offer to him, how our mouths speak and sing and shout, where our feet take us, the tears we shed on his feet and the hair with which we wipe them up, the river we wash ourselves in, the symbols of his body and blood we ingest, the dances we embarrass ourselves with in his presence, and much, much more.

Like Charapas acting out a story, we are to act out our relationship with God. The life of faith is to be lived, not contemplated. We need to be attentive to the possibility that our mouths say one thing to God while our actions say another.

Biblical prayers begin with *im*pressions, but they usually end with *ex*pressions, and at some point the inside and the outside are supposed to match. Visible, expressive prayer often integrates our body and soul and brings them together. If our prayers don't involve our senses, they don't involve the whole person. Since God never desires less than everything, give him your heart. Make it real. Or else forget about it.

# LISTEN WITH YOUR EYES

## A 20/20 Conversation

"I turned to see the voice that was speaking to me."[71] That's what John said when Jesus spoke to him on Patmos with a voice like a trumpet. John wanted to "see" the sound.

It's easy to read that line simply as a figure of speech. What John really meant, of course, was that he turned to see who was speaking. Obviously, you can't see a voice, can you? Then again, John was entering into a supernatural experience where he tried desperately to describe the scenes of heaven in terms of the finest gems and metals on earth. He saw angelic creatures with four faces, elders who fell down frequently before the throne, bowls of incense, bowls of wrath, and Babylon and the beast. He also heard voices of thunder and waterfalls, songs and shouts of multitudes, great roars, and angelic proclamations. He smelled incense and tasted a scroll that was sweet to the mouth and bitter to the stomach.

John got caught up in a mind-blowing experience that would leave any of us scrambling for words. We can forgive him for saying he turned to "see" the voice. Considering the situation, that wasn't an unreasonable statement to make.

Regardless of whether we want to read that strange phrase literally, it's an apt description of what it's like to listen to God. Listening, after all, is an integral part of prayer. And when we listen for God's voice, we don't exactly tune our ears to the sounds in the sky. We watch for shifts in our circumstances or signs that we've requested. We keep our eyes and ears open for Bible verses, phrases from sermons, and friendly counsel that might reflect his guidance. The prophet Habakkuk expressed the same dynamic when he said, "I will keep watch to *see* what He will speak to me and how I may reply."[72] Interaction with God is often visual. When we listen—and, we may assume, when we speak back to him—any voices involved often require an attentive eye. That's the nature of divine, multidimensional communication.

*Listening is an integral part of prayer.*

Visual communication is commonplace in the Bible, and it goes both ways—from God to us and from us to God. God didn't just thunder his words to Abraham, as far as we know. Sometimes an angel spoke from heaven,[73] sometimes God appeared to Abraham in a vision,[74] and sometimes he showed up as a humanlike visitor.[75]

When God gave Abraham a promise, he showed Abraham the stars in the sky and the sand on the ground and told him his descendants would be as numerous as each. When God made a covenant with Abraham, he cut a deal—literally. Several animal carcasses were split in half and set opposite each other in a line. But unlike the usual custom of both parties walking between them to signify a blood covenant, God did this one unilaterally—with "great darkness," a smoking oven, and a flaming torch.[76] Those are pretty strong images.

Abraham spoke to God in visual terms too. Nearly everywhere he went, he built an altar to worship God or to stake his claim in God-given territory.[77] Once he planted a tamarisk tree in the place where he called on the Lord.[78] When the priest of Salem, Melchizedek, came to Abraham after a victory in battle, he brought bread and wine, and Abraham ate a very symbolic meal that would point to another High Priest centuries later.[79] Clearly, God was establishing "multimedia" communication with the father of faith.

*When God spoke through Ezekiel,*
*he spoke in pictures.*

In Ezekiel's prophecies, God spoke visually by telling the prophet to act out his messages. He told Ezekiel to make a brick model of the siege of Jerusalem, for example, and then lie on his left side for 390 days (one day for each year of Israel's sin) and on his right side for forty days (one day for each year of Judah's sin). In another act, he had to shave his hair and divide it into three piles, each pile representing a third of Israel. One bunch of hair was to be burned, one to be cut with a sword, and the other to be scattered in the wind. But a small remnant was to be sewn into his garment because a remnant of Israel would be spared. For still another image, he was told to cook his bread over dung to represent the thorough corruption and consequences of sin.[80] When God spoke through Ezekiel, he spoke in pictures.

He did the same with Zechariah. He could have given Zechariah a simple message: "Tell Zerubbabel that his strength is in my Spirit, not in his military power."

But no, in Zechariah 4, he sent an angel to say, "What do you see?" and a lengthy interchange began.

Zechariah described a vision of a lamp stand with an olive tree on each side, a picture of the Spirit and his anointed ones. "What are these?" he asked.

"Do you not know what these are?"

"No, my lord."

"This is the word of the LORD to Zerubbabel," the angel said. "'Not by might nor by power, but by My Spirit,' says the LORD of hosts."

This kind of interaction continues through many of the visions, with Zechariah saying, "What's this?" about each element and the angel responding, "You don't know?"

Yes, God could have spoken the truth and the application to Zechariah, but he didn't. He showed a graphic picture that would stick in his memory and have biblical scholars plumbing the depths of it for centuries to come.

But even when divine communication is verbal, it can be highly visual. Jesus gave quite a few graphic illustrations, like saying that we should rather gouge out a sinful eye than risk ending up in hell for it, that love looks like a repugnant Samaritan going out of his way to nurse the wounds of another and pay his medical bills, or that unresponsive people are like seeds sown on rocky soil. Though only words rather than a prophetic vision, such illustrations are more picturesque than verbal. Jesus used them a lot.

Once when I was reading through the prophets, I tried to highlight every metaphor I saw. By the time I was done, at least three-quarters of most pages were colored with my blue or yellow highlights. It would have been easier to highlight the verses that *didn't* have pictorial metaphors. The language God inspired his communicators to use was deeply symbolic, highly visual, and broadly sensory. Take, for example, this graphic and disturbing passage from Ezekiel, and see how many times the prophet appeals to your senses of sight, taste, touch, and smell:

Thus says the Lord GOD to Jerusalem, "Your origin and your birth are from the land of the Canaanite, your father was an Amorite and your mother a Hittite. As for your birth, on the day you were born your navel cord was not cut, nor were you washed with water for cleansing; you were not rubbed with salt or even wrapped in cloths. No eye looked with pity on you to do any of these things for you, to have compassion on you. Rather you were thrown out into the open field, for you were abhorred on the day you were born.

"When I passed by you and saw you squirming in your blood, I said to you while you were in your blood, 'Live!' Yes, I said to you while you were in your blood, 'Live!' I made you numerous like plants of the field. Then you grew up, became tall and reached the age for fine ornaments; your breasts were formed and your hair had grown. Yet you were naked and bare.

"Then I passed by you and saw you, and behold, you were at the time for love; so I spread My skirt over you and covered your nakedness. I also swore to you and entered into a covenant with you so that you became Mine," declares the Lord GOD. "Then I bathed you with water, washed off your blood from you and anointed you with oil. I also clothed you with embroidered cloth and put sandals of porpoise skin on your feet; and I wrapped you with fine linen and covered you with silk. I adorned you with ornaments, put bracelets on your hands and a necklace around your neck. I also put a ring in your nostril, earrings in your ears and a beautiful crown on your head. Thus you were adorned with gold and silver, and your dress was of fine linen, silk and embroidered cloth. You ate fine flour, honey and oil; so you were exceedingly beautiful and advanced to royalty. Then your fame went forth among the nations on account of your beauty, for it was perfect because of My splendor which I bestowed on you," declares the Lord GOD.

"But you trusted in your beauty and played the harlot because of your fame, and you poured out your harlotries on every passer-by who might be willing. You took some of your clothes, made for yourself high places of various colors and played the harlot on them, which should never come about nor happen. You also took your beautiful jewels made of My gold and of My silver, which I had given you, and made for yourself male images that you might play the harlot with them. Then you took your embroidered cloth and covered them, and offered My oil and My incense before them. Also My bread which I gave you, fine flour, oil and honey with which I fed you, you would offer before them for a soothing aroma; so it happened," declares the Lord GOD. "Moreover, you took your sons and daughters whom you had borne to Me and sacrificed them to idols to be devoured. Were your harlotries so small a matter? You slaughtered My children and offered them up to idols by causing them to pass through the fire. Besides all your abominations and harlotries you did not remember the days of your youth, when you were naked and bare and squirming in your blood....

"How languishing is your heart," declares the Lord GOD, "while you do all these things, the actions of a bold-faced harlot. When you built your shrine at the beginning of every street and made your high place in every square, in disdaining money, you were not like a harlot. You adulteress wife, who takes strangers instead of her husband!"[81]

That passage would be remarkable except that it's only one among hundreds in which biblical terminology paints a picture or recruits the reader's senses of smell, taste, and touch. This is not isolated language.

Prayer in this context is holistic. God causes us to visualize his words. In turn, we who reflect his image can do the same. He certainly doesn't mind if we visualize or portray our words to him. He has made it clear that he enjoys this kind of language. He loves metaphors and invites us to use them.

Our normal approach in prayer is to envision what we would like him to do and then describe it in English or whatever language we speak best. Sometimes we even itemize a step-by-step answer for him, something along the lines of, "Lord, in order for you to answer this petition, here's what needs to happen. ..." Then we list it for him, in case he needs our problem-solving advice. Our prayers turn into micromanagement as we cover every detail of the plan he should follow. We pray an instruction manual.

Jesus told us to pray that God's kingdom would come, that his will would be done on earth as it is in heaven. In order to obey that instruction, we have to know something about his kingdom—its culture, its values, the character of its King, and so on. So, having already told his disciples to pray "thy kingdom come," how did he

teach them what it should look like? With a list of kingdom prior-
ities? A detailed description of its characteristics? The discipleship
employee handbook? No, in the parables he gave them pictures like
this:

- "The kingdom of heaven is like a man who sowed good
  seed in his field..."[82]
- "The kingdom of heaven is like a mustard seed..."[83]
- "The kingdom of heaven is like leaven..."[84]
- "The kingdom of heaven is like a treasure hidden in the
  field..."[85]
- "The kingdom of heaven is like a merchant seeking fine
  pearls..."[86]
- "The kingdom of heaven is like a dragnet cast into the
  sea..."[87]
- "The kingdom of heaven is like a king who wanted to settle
  accounts with his servants..."[88]
- "The kingdom of heaven is like a landowner who went out
  early in the morning to hire laborers for his vineyard..."[89]
- "The kingdom of heaven is like a king who prepared a wedding banquet for his son..."[90]
- "The kingdom of heaven will be like ten virgins who took
  their lamps and went out to meet the bridegroom..."[91]

Are these snapshots of the kingdom given simply to inform and
motivate the disciples? Maybe. But Jesus had already made it clear
that they were to pray for the kingdom to be made manifest around
them, here on earth. Could these kingdom portraits be clues showing them how they should pray? I think so. They are powerful pictures that specifically tie in to the prayer life of the disciples. They
were given so that kingdom followers would be able to envision what
they were praying for.

## PRAY YOUR VISION

There's nothing wrong with describing our desires to God, but why do we even bother with that step? We already have a mental picture. Why not present it to him directly? If a picture is worth a thousand words, why fumble around with a thousand words? It's like e-mailing someone a long description of the gorgeous landscape you saw on your vacation, when all the while you have a digital picture that you could attach and send. If you're worried that God doesn't understand the pictures in your heart, you've forgotten that his native language isn't English, Greek, Hebrew, or whatever. Most often in his Word, he "speaks" in pictures. You can too.

My wife, Hannah, reminded me of this recently, although she had no idea that's what she was doing. We were on the ministry team at church that week, which means we stood up at the front after the service in case anybody needed to pray with someone. A man came up for prayer and told us that he was concerned for his wife, who was a believer but was very far from God and not living the truths of the gospel. The wife seemed to have no interest in spiritual matters anymore.

As the ministry-team husband, I felt I should take the lead and pray first. I prayed that God would rekindle this woman's love for Jesus, that he would show his favor to her and remind her of how much he loves her, that she would become sensitive again to the work of his Spirit, and on and on in that vein—which was some pretty good praying, if you ask me.

Then Hannah took her turn. "Lord, I see you putting a target on her heart, and I see every word that you speak to her hitting the bull's-eye. So I just ask you to do that. Shoot arrows of your grace and compassion into her."

*Well, yeah,* I thought, *I guess that about sums it up. Not sure why I didn't think of that. Sure would have been easier. Probably more powerful too.*

One time during the worship portion of a church service, Timothy, my seven-year-old, was running around in one corner of the auditorium acting like he was shooting people with an invisible squirt gun. Worship time in our church is very informal, and there's a lot of freedom for people to do whatever they feel led to do, so his activity didn't bother me. His motive, however, did. Like a good dad, I told him he needed to spend this time focusing on God and not pretending to assault helpless worshipers with invisible weaponry.

"But Dad," he said innocently, "I'm spraying people with Jesus' love! Every time I squeeze my spray bottle, I see his love sprinkling all over people."

"Oh," I muttered. "Well, carry on, then."

Timothy ran off excitedly to continue his mission.

If Timothy's spiritual development were entirely in my hands without the Holy Spirit's frequent intervention, I'd probably teach him to pray that people would be open to receiving God's love and that they would understand how much he loves them. I'd explain to him that deep down everyone craves the love of their Creator, but there are so many obstacles in the way that they have a hard time recognizing their desire. I'd teach him to plead with God to remove those obstacles and show them his love clearly. I'd give him a lot of words to describe the process. Thank God that Timothy's spiritual development isn't entirely in my hands.

It isn't that my prayers along those lines aren't good. They're very consistent with God's purposes. But didn't Timothy have a great picture of Jesus' love that captured God's heart better than my many words did? Maybe this is one of the reasons Jesus said we have to have the faith of a child. A child can run around spraying people with God's love and count it as prayer. And if any Sunday school teacher ever came along and told Timothy that's not a real prayer, he or she would have to put some gloves on and go a couple of rounds with me. My son can present that picture to his Father any time he wants to. And I'm absolutely certain that his Father accepts that picture as a prayer request.

## THE KINGDOM OR A CULT?

In the Bible, visions are the language of the seer. In fact, that's why prophets are called seers. They see things. Throughout Scripture, God seems to be pretty comfortable with his people seeing things, either in outward visions or in inward thoughts. New Age mysticism did not come up with this concept. Corrupted it, maybe, but it was in the heart of God before paganism co-opted it.

Still, many Christians are skeptical of the role of imagination in prayer. It's seen as an occultish sort of practice—Christian shamanism is one way I've heard it described. Before getting into a discussion on that, let me first pose this challenge: try praying for something *without* picturing it in your mind. You won't be able to do it. The mind is crafted for images, and you can't speak or even think without them. People who say that visualizing has no place in Christian spirituality have a really hard time living up to their ideal. We can't *stop* imagining; this is how we think. We have images passing through our minds all day long.

*People who say that visualizing has no place in Christian spirituality have a really hard time living up to their ideal.*

Where we differ from New Age practices and Eastern mysticism is that we submit our minds to God and allow him to inspire the images. We don't believe that whatever comes into our minds can become reality if we just think it and believe it hard enough. We do believe, however, that the Holy Spirit actually has some influence over our yielded thoughts and enjoys using them to give us pictures of his will and his kingdom. If he didn't take pleasure in that, he wouldn't have put so many images in his Word.

The Bible practically begs us to envision the kingdom, to get excited about it, and to pray for it to come on earth as it is in heaven. It gives us pictures of heaven so we'll know how to hope in Christ. The promises of God are not spelled out for us in a legal document. They are embodied in the lives of real people in real time in real places in history. That's what our Scripture is all about.

And this is why the New Testament writers urge us to be spiritually discerning. They focus on the message, not the medium. Nowhere does Scripture tell us all visions or pictorial thoughts are bad; it tells us to distinguish which ones are from God. In fact, God doesn't just tolerate our imaginations. He *wants* our minds to be filled with images—*his* images, like a sower spreading his seed, a father running out to meet a returning prodigal, a shepherd searching for his sheep, the lion and the lamb lying down together, the resurrected Jesus standing in heaven with flaming eyes and golden clothes and glory all around. He drew up the tabernacle and temple, with all their measurements and materials, as symbolic images of the salvation to come, so that when Jews pictured them in their minds, they would think of the truth of the Messiah. He painted the Passover celebration as a graphic depiction of the cross. We simply can't read the Scriptures without forming mental images, and we can't pray without forming them either. God interacts with us in the pictures of the mind. He always has.

So how do we communicate visually with God? How about asking him to engage us in that kind of conversation? We ask him for other kinds of guidance with the expectation he'll give it. Why limit the media through which he speaks?

*Why limit the media through which he speaks?*

A frequent rebuttal to such questioning is that God speaks through his Word and *only* through his Word. While we can be certain that God will not contradict his Word in the ways he speaks to us, nearly all who claim that his only mode of expression is printed words on the Bible's pages are not being honest with themselves.

How do I know? Because nearly every Christian is willing to accept the testimony of a pastor who says he was called into ministry through a combination of personal convictions, open doors of circumstances, the affirmation of others, and the inward guidance of the Holy Spirit. Nearly every Christian will attribute guidance to God when it comes in the form of an inward push or an inner peace, the counsel of godly people in conjunction with open or closed doors of opportunity, or a phrase in a conversation that seems to speak louder than the amplifiers at a rock concert and comes at exactly the right time.

Again, we wouldn't follow any guidance that contradicts Scripture, because we know that's not from God. But we've already opened the doors of our hearts to biblical principles of counsel and accountability, circumstances and opportunities, personal convictions and the inner witness of the Holy Spirit. Those can be pretty subjective media, but when we submit them to the authority of God, ask him to lead us, trust that he will do so, and see that the guidance seems to converge in one specific direction, we feel pretty safe that we've heard his voice.

So we've clearly opened the doors of revelation beyond just the written Word. Why not go ahead and open up to the possibility that he can guide the mental images we already can't avoid having? We know how to ask God to guide our thoughts and feelings. Why not ask him to guide our imaginations?

Again, yes, that can be subjective. So can the piercing statement in a sermon that cuts to the heart, or the "peace that passes all understanding," or any other communication we receive from God. But if we don't think he's willing to assist our spiritual vision, we've got a pretty strange doctrine of the Holy Spirit. Jesus promised that he would guide us. It just isn't consistent to rule the imagination out of our fellowship with him.

When God gives us what may be a mental picture of his will, we have every right—even an obligation—to present it to him as a prayer. How does this work? Next time you envision a scenario you think is God's will, pray this: *Lord, as far as I can tell, this picture in my mind comes from you and would honor you if fulfilled. I submit it to you to accept it, deny it, alter it, or whatever you want to do. But if it's your will, please imprint it deeper on my mind and in my heart so I can believe it fully. And please bring it to pass.*

> When God gives us what may be a mental picture of his will, we have every right—even an obligation—to present it to him as a prayer.

That's not a bad prayer at all. It isn't unbiblical either. We can either describe that scenario to God in words and ask him to fulfill it, or we can say, "Hey, you see this picture in my mind? That's what I'm praying." Either way, we're offering him the same request. The difference is that one way can get us bogged down in faith-killing details. The other can make our hearts beat faster and inspire us to hope.

## EXCHANGING PICTURES

Pictures change lives. That's why Jesus depended so much on parables and preachers depend so much on illustrations. Simply explaining abstract thoughts doesn't connect with the human spirit. We receive truth only when we see its importance or how it might apply to our lives. Pictures pierce the heart in ways that explanations can't.

In response to God's gift of images to illuminate his truth, many biblical prayers return the favor. Hannah, for example, didn't just tell God thank you when he answered her prayer for a son. She exploded into pictorial praise: her "horn" was exalted, there was no "rock" like her God, the bows of the warriors were broken, the satisfied found themselves looking for bread, the needy were lifted from the ash heap and seated with princes, and God thundered from heaven.[92] As far as I can tell from reading Hannah's story—how she prayed for a son, and the priest assured her that her prayer would be answered—there were no bows and arrows involved. The nobles weren't humiliated and the needy weren't placed in royal courts. And there was no thunder from heaven. But in Hannah's heart, all those images were being displayed. To her, this answered petition was a monumental victory as stirring as the Exodus or the conquest of Canaan. In her prayer, she spoke in pictures. And I strongly suspect she wasn't sitting still.

*Prayer seems to have its own landscape and is not confined to the cosmos as we know it.*

We also see this kind of pictorial prayer often in the psalms, and it starts early. In the first psalm, for example, the righteous are like a tree firmly planted by streams of water, and the wicked are like chaff driven away by the wind. Not long after, David speaks to God as his "shield" and the One who shatters the teeth of his enemies.[93] Throughout the prayers of the psalmists, God is a warrior, he rides on the clouds, he hides us in cliffs and caves, and we thirst for him like a deer pants for water. Prayer seems to have its own landscape and is not confined to the cosmos as we know it.

One of the most familiar examples of pictorial prayer is Psalm 23, which, if I had written it, probably would have looked like this:

The Lord takes care of me, so I won't lack anything.
I can rest securely and be refreshed.
He teaches me the right things to do so I won't embarrass
     him.
Even when I feel like I'm going to die,
I don't have to be afraid of evil.
You will comfort me, Lord.
You feed me, bless me, and give me victory in abundance.
Your love goes with me everywhere,
And I'll live with you forever.

Now that's a nice little prayer, but it's pretty boring, and an hour later I would probably forget that I prayed it. Plus, I can pray those words with my brain tied behind my back; I don't have to engage intellectually or emotionally to say them. It contains truths I've known since I was little. I could move my lips to that prayer without meaning a word of it.

You're probably familiar with how David wrote it. The Lord is a Shepherd who takes care of his sheep, who gives them safe pasture next to soothing waters. Even when his sheep have to walk through life-threatening valleys, he's there with them to guide and protect. He honors them with a banquet in front of the wolves that want to eat them for dinner. He brings them out safely and gives them far more than any sheep ever deserved. And they end up in his house forever.

Now that's a prayer in God's native language. It's poetic and picturesque, and it communicates more truth than any abstract explanation ever could. I think we can safely assume that your pastor isn't going to preach this Sunday on the prayer as I've written it. But I wouldn't bet against his preaching on David's version. Whole libraries could be filled with the texts of sermons about the Twenty-Third Psalm. It's rich and powerful. You can't come up with that kind of prayer if you aren't fully engaged intellectually and emotionally. It's fertile, personal communication between the human and divine.

*Prayer is a vital, living organism, filled with purpose and poetry.*

That's the kind of example God gives us repeatedly in Scripture. Prayer is a vital, living organism, filled with purpose and poetry. It isn't creative simply for the sake of creativity; it's creative because communication with an infinite God stretches us beyond mere words. It makes us long for voices that can be seen.

# Six

# EMOTIONAL PRAYER

## The Pitfalls of Vulcan Christianity

Chris, if your spiritual life is based on your emotions, you'll be up one day and down the next," my discipleship group leader told me. "It's like basing your marriage on infatuation. You'd be in love and out of love more times than you can imagine. Commitments don't fluctuate. Discipleship isn't about how you feel."

That sounded like good advice, so I took it. I didn't want to live a roller-coaster life, so for years I tried to eliminate emotions from my relationship with God. I would tell myself that the desires of my heart were irrelevant, that all my decisions needed to be based on my understanding of truth alone, and that any negative emotions like anger or grief were unspiritual. It didn't take long before I began to feel like an utter spiritual failure—though that feeling wasn't legitimate, I told myself. And I really did accomplish my goal of avoiding a roller-coaster life. I was always low and never high. I felt completely disconnected from God.

The advice I got from my leader had some truth in it, and it was reinforced numerous times over the years. I can't count the number of times I've heard a sermon telling me that faith is not a feeling. I've heard just as many telling me the same thing about love. I've even preached those truths. Our spiritual attributes are based on facts, we tell ourselves. When we make them emotional, they become inconsistent.

That's true at a fundamental level, but it's a horrible way to live. The principle that our love and faith are matters of truth is only part of the story. Try, for example, telling your spouse something like this: "Honey, I just want you to know that our marriage isn't based on feelings. I love you because of that marriage certificate we signed." But don't say that unless you enjoy sleeping on the couch. Yes, you'd make the point that your commitment is constant. Before long, however, your relationship would die.

So why do we think our discipleship can be governed by that principle? Because we overreact to the other extreme: emotionalism. We've seen people get caught up in the emotions of a church service and make a commitment that's only skin deep. We know people who are great followers of Jesus on the mountaintop and card-carrying pagans in the valley. We don't want our discipleship to look like that, so we preach and teach that emotions are unreliable. Our over-emphasis on that point implies that feelings will only hinder our growth, so we should always ignore them.

*Overreaction to emotionalism damages the image of God.*

But this overreaction to emotionalism damages the image of God. He gave each of us a mind, a will, and emotions, and we turn our discipleship into a two-out-of-three endeavor. When our thoughts don't conform to the image of Christ, we seek to transform them. When our will, or our behavior, doesn't conform to the image of Christ, we seek to transform it. But when our feelings don't conform to the image of Christ, we tell ourselves they are irrelevant and push them aside. And the Spirit who hovered over dust—who breathed into us a mind, will, *and* emotions—is grieved.

## VULCAN CHRISTIANITY

In the original *Star Trek* series, Mr. Spock always made decisions based entirely on logic. That's because he was half Vulcan, and Vulcans don't have emotions. Spock was portrayed as somewhat of an ideal, a valuable member of the crew because he didn't let feelings get in the way of doing the right thing.

Spock's exclusively logical approach to life found its ultimate expression in one of the Star Trek movies made years after the series. In the climactic battle in *The Wrath of Khan,* the main engine of the starship *Enterprise* is disabled, and the ship appears unable to escape an impending explosion. But Spock forces his way into the ship's reactor room and, fully exposed to lethal streams of radiation, repairs the engine. When his old friend Kirk comes to the window of the reactor room, Spock looks out and explains that it was logical for one to die for the many. Then he dies, and the ship is able to speed away to safety.

Many Christians think that's how Jesus went to the cross. It was a cold, calculated, reasonable thing to do. After all, his night in Gethsemane makes it clear that he didn't *feel* like enduring the agony. And Scripture even affirms that it's "logical" for one man to die so that many can live.[94] But if we asked the writer of Hebrews why Jesus really chose to sacrifice himself, we might be surprised at how this inspired author describes the Savior's inward motivation. He endured the cross "for the *joy* set before Him."[95]

> *Jesus chose the cross because of the joy it would lead to. He wanted to.*

That's right. If Jesus didn't feel like going to the cross the night he was arrested, why did he? For joy. An emotion. He didn't replace his emotions with logic; he replaced them with a deeper, better, truer, longer-lasting emotion. Yes, his sacrifice was logical, but logic doesn't really motivate us. It only has the power to prompt a person to do something reluctantly. Jesus, apparently, didn't go to the cross reluctantly. He chose it because of the joy it would lead to. He wanted to.

Most of current discipleship training emphasizes the transformation of the mind and the will. When, for example, have you ever heard a preacher talk about how vital it is to share God's feelings? I've never heard that idea coming from a pulpit. It's all about what we understand and how we act.

I think this has created a generation of Vulcan Christians—disciples who live entirely out of their minds and their willful behavior, dismissing the value of emotions. The result is either intellectualism or legalism, neither of which makes life very enjoyable. Yes, we avoid emotionalism, but we sacrifice part of our soul. We may end up looking like disciples that way—I certainly did—but we don't really connect with God. And as with a marriage based entirely on a certificate, our love for him begins to die.

If you've traveled that route, you understand that willpower Christianity won't get you very far. If your discipleship is invested entirely in your mind and your will, not only do you never really connect with God relationally, you also burn out in a hurry. Willpower doesn't bear the fruit of the Spirit (which, by the way, is pretty emotional fruit: love, joy, peace, patience, kindness, and so on[96]), and it doesn't last—just note your progress on that last New Year's resolution, for example. The only time willpower is effective is when it's accompanied by strong motivation. And motivation, it should be noted, comes from the same root as the word *emotion*. It's no coincidence that we describe our emotional moments as being moved. That's where motivation comes from. Without it, discipleship is dead in the water.

Why is this important to a discussion on creativity? Because emotions are the fuel for imaginative expression. Creativity doesn't come out of faith that has turned cerebral or legalistic; people haven't ever created great works of art purely from the mind or the will. They may have created on commission, but their creativity didn't flow from the prospect of getting paid. It flowed out of their past experiences and the emotions that surrounded those experiences.

> *Creative expression involves the mind and the will, but it grows in the fertile soil of human feelings.*

Yes, most of the greatest music, literature, and art the world has ever seen or heard came into being because someone felt something deeply. Creative expression involves the mind and the will, but it grows in the fertile soil of human feelings. Without emotions, our expression is lifeless and empty. With emotions, it becomes imaginative, vibrant, and zealous. And very creative.

## How God Breathed

Let's return to that scene in Eden, where lifeless dust was filled with the Breath of God. That dust became the image of the Creator—who, by the way, was very emotional and enthusiastic about what he had made, as evidenced by the repeated expressions of his satisfaction: he saw that "it was good," and he saw that "it was *very* good."[97]

We may have been conditioned over the years to read God's "it was good" statements of Genesis 1 in the tone of voice of a builder who says, "This will suffice," but the text is more emotional than that.[98] God was excited about his work, like a painter who puts the finishing touches on his greatest masterpiece and keenly anticipates the rave reviews it will receive. When the Breath of God blew into this very good image of himself, what did the image contain? A body, a spirit, and, somewhere in between, a soul that includes a mind, a will, and a wide range of emotions.

This God-likeness means that we have emotions because God gave them to us—from his own personality. Theology deals with God's emotions awkwardly because of our frame of reference. Our experience with feelings is that they are inconsistent and frequently reactions of surprise, and we know God isn't inconsistent or surprised about anything. But as much as theologians have trouble with the concept of a God who has feelings, the Bible is full of references to them. His own revelation portrays him with these emotions:

- *delight:* He delights in rewarding obedience (and disobedience),[99] in uprightness,[100] in righteous sacrifices,[101] in his wisdom,[102] in fair and faithful people,[103] in the prayers of the upright,[104] in his chosen people,[105] in his own attributes of lovingkindness, justice, and righteousness,[106] and in loyalty.[107]

- *anger:* God's anger is expressed often, especially in the prophets, in response to disobedience, faithlessness, and stubbornness. Scripture even uses extreme terms, describing his "fierce anger,"[108] "burning anger,"[109] and "hot displeasure."[110]

- *love:* God's love in Scripture frequently has emotional overtones,[111] and though Jesus certainly loved all his disciples, John is distinguished as the disciple "whom Jesus loved"[112]—implying a deeper emotional response to John than to the others.

- *jealousy:* We consider jealousy to be sinful by nature, but God doesn't—at least when godly principles are involved. He tells us his name is "Jealous,"[113] his jealousy is a consuming fire,[114] and he is "exceedingly jealous" for Jerusalem and Zion.[115] In all, the kind of jealousy a scorned lover might have is explicitly ascribed to God at least twenty-six times in Scripture.

- *hate:* God is love, but he also hates. He hates idolatry;[116] violence;[117] pride, deceit, injustice, wicked plans, slander, and strife;[118] meaningless rituals and ceremonies;[119] divorce;[120] and the multitude of acts and attitudes described in Scripture as an "abomination."

- *joy:* "The LORD takes pleasure in His people."[121] He also rejoices with his people in the victories he wins for them.[122] Jesus himself marveled when he saw great faith,[123] he depicted a wild celebration in heaven when a sinner repents,[124] and he portrayed the Father as a party-thrower because a prodigal returned.[125]

- *grief:* Frequently in Scripture, God grieved over the sin and lostness of his people. Jesus lamented over Jerusalem,[126]

and Paul made it clear that the Spirit—the Breath of
God—can be grieved.[127]

- *zeal:* God does all things well. He does some things,
  however, with extra enthusiasm or zeal: preserving Judah's
  remnant,[128] battling for his people,[129] accomplishing righteousness and salvation,[130] and expressing his wrath.[131]
  When Jesus cleansed the temple by overthrowing the tables
  of the money-changers, he fulfilled a prophecy by demon-
  strating zeal for his Father's house.[132]

Clearly, the Bible portrays God as extremely emotional. I find it
encouraging that two emotions are never assigned to him: those
that fall under the category of fear (anxiety, worry, stress) and
those that fall under the category of despair (discouragement, apa-
thy, depression, hopelessness). We should give these feelings no
place in our hearts. They are not in line with God's emotions.

But what about the others? Is there a place in discipleship for our
emotions to conform to God's? For us to be angry where he is angry,
jealous where he is jealous, joyful where he is joyful, and so on? If the
Breath of God blew his own image into the Adam of creation, then
he meant for emotions not to be dismissed by human beings, but to
be fulfilled in them. He meant for our hearts to beat with his.

## God's Heartbeat

This is where we bond with God—or anyone else, for that matter.
We don't connect with people over information or circumstances,
but rather over emotional responses to information or circumstances. We get to know friends and loved ones only when we see
how they respond to the situations of life—especially how they
respond emotionally. When you see someone's tears welling up at a

movie or during a song, you learn something about his or her sensitivities. If those line up with your sensitivities, you connect. If they don't, you don't.

*Our connection with God depends on sharing emotions with him.*

Our connection with God depends on sharing emotions with him. We're born of his Spirit and being conformed to the image of Christ. His Spirit, according to the Bible, has a full range of emotions, and so does Jesus. If we are filled with his Breath and following Christ, we will bond with God emotionally. And if we bond with him emotionally, our expressions toward him will reflect that.

Misunderstanding the role and the legitimacy of emotions has resulted in many people feeling detached from God, the way I did when I tried to overrule my emotions at all times. When we operate under a model of discipleship that says feelings are irrelevant, we drain ourselves of the fuel that motivates us. It's like spraying a potent herbicide over the whole lawn. Yes, it kills the weeds, but it also ruins the purpose of the lawn. You end up with an awfully bare landscape.

Many Christians are following Jesus across an awfully bare landscape. I know because I've been there; I've sprayed poisons over the very desires God has placed within my heart. I've drained myself of the things God was using to motivate me, and I ended up lifeless. I found that without emotions, my mind and my will have no power.

We don't have to look far in Scripture to find emotional prayers. We've already mentioned Hannah, who was so recklessly expressive in her prayer that the priest thought she was drunk.[133] Hezekiah tore his clothes in distress and went into the house of the Lord when he heard of the taunts of an invading king,[134] and he wept bitterly when he prayed for God to heal him of a fatal disease.[135] David screamed some of his prayers, argued in some, and danced in others.

And if we really want an irrefutable example, here's how Jesus' prayers are described: "He offered up both prayers and supplications with loud crying and tears to the One able to save Him from death, and He was heard because of His piety."[136] Did you catch that? Scripture associates loud crying and tears with piety. If Jesus wore his emotions on his sleeve when he talked with the Father, so can we.

*The psalms are full of emotional prayer.*

The psalms are full of emotional prayer. In fact, it's hard to find a psalm that isn't laced with intense feelings and creative expressions that flow out of those feelings. Usually, those feelings are right in line with God's own heart. When they aren't, they usually conform to him by the end of the psalm. The psalms contain prayers that are violent and visceral, exuberant and exhilarating, passionate and pointed. The extremes of human emotion are in them, and God responds to them without rebuke. He doesn't just tolerate our feelings; he *desires* them.

We therefore see fiery prophetic pictures from Isaiah to Malachi. When Jeremiah said the word of God burned within him,[137] he didn't just mean he had information to share. His bones were boiling with a feverish urge that simply could not contain God's message. That's what happens when the emotions of an infinite God are poured into a finite soul. It's a volcano waiting to erupt. Like the picture in Ezekiel 16 of God the faithful husband grieving over Israel the unfaithful whore, expression between God and humanity is meant to ooze from the heart's deepest impulses.

In light of the fact that God is burning with jealousy for his people, is fuming over sin, is weeping over those ignorant of him, and is celebrating over the thousands of people who came to him in faith today, is there any reason for us to think he expects us to pray emotionless, dignified prayers? When we see this imbalance in a human relationship—a highly expressive man married to an unexpressive, monotonous wife, or vice versa—we wonder if the couple is compatible. Is there any reason to think God desires an emotionally unbalanced relationship with us? Or would it perhaps be better to assume that if he sets an emotional tone bursting with creative expression, then he wants us to conform to it?

## RAW AND REAL

Many Christians are afraid of this kind of prayer. It's too raw and too real. It contradicts some traditional models of prayer, like the monastic model of stripping oneself of personality and emotion to get calm and contemplative before God, the severity of Puritanism, or the quiet, inward piety of the early missionary movement.[138] It also runs against the stream of contemporary discipleship programs, as discussed above. But it doesn't contradict Scripture at all; in fact, it fits the biblical models of prayer better than it fits those that church history has produced. There are enormous emotional swings in Scripture, and God not only tolerates them, he participates in them. We dismiss them to our own detriment.

If you have felt suppressed in your prayers, feeling that you have to dispense with your true feelings to come into the sobering, dispassionate presence of God, let me encourage you to be free of that false assumption. God does not suppress your emotions, and he doesn't ask you to suppress them either. He does want them conformed to the feelings of his heart—that's a given. Not every emotion that spills out of us is worth spilling, as some of them can be rather ugly. But God will help the transformation process. As your heart draws near to his, its rhythm will begin to synchronize with his.

> *God does not suppress your emotions,*
> *and he doesn't ask you*
> *to suppress them either.*

Look at it this way: Would you rather read a movie script, or watch the movie? Listen to an audio book read by a monotone narrator, or by a professional actor and accompanied by background music and sound effects? Have your child present you with a Christmas wish list, or see him overflow with enthusiasm for a particular desire? If people like us, who have only five senses and a limited array of emotions, would prefer the options with more personality in them, what do you think the God who has infinite senses and emotions would prefer?

When you pray, understand that emotionless prayers are like reading a script to God. He'll get the information—he already knows it, in fact—but you won't bond with him in the process. Like a Vulcan, you'll operate logically and methodically, and you'll begin to feel as if God is doing the same with you, even though he never has and never will. You'll become a disciple of Spock who makes sacrifices not for the joy set before him, but because you've deadened your feelings by calling them irrelevant. And you'll miss out on the richness and fullness of a relationship with a very personal, emotional God.

God doesn't ask you to do that, despite what traditional prayer models may have tried to tell you. Prayers without emotions are not authentic, and they'll never become creative or imaginative in their expression. A disciple without strong emotions is a robot, not a disciple. The God who breathed passionately and creatively into his handiwork long ago hopes for that passionate Breath to be expressed in a two-way relationship. It's the only way to be conformed to the image of a Savior whose grief was overshadowed by the joy set before him.

# Seven

# TANGIBLE PRAYER

## When Words Are Not Enough

The worship team had finished practicing, and the room was filled with expectant people. Many of them had come a long way to receive ministry in our Friday night service, and we didn't want them to go home disappointed. But there was one critical problem: we were sitting in darkness.

A thunderstorm had just moved through the area and caused a transformer to blow. The whole neighborhood was dark. (We found out later that it wasn't just our neighborhood; a large area of the city had been affected.) The electric company would have its hands full for a while.

We found some flashlights and lit some candles, but that solved only part of the problem. The worship leaders were prepared to lead us in a solid hour of worship, but they depended completely on electricity. There's usually an acoustic guitar somewhere in the building, but not that night. It looked as if our leaders would have to be more creative than usual.

Johnny, our pastor, went to his office, pulled out his shofar—a ram's horn referred to in Scripture as a trumpet—and walked to the front of the room.

"Lord, send your angels to help us!" he shouted with a playful, let's-see-if-this-works smile on his face. And he blew the shofar as loudly as he could.

Within three seconds, the lights came on—not the lights in the neighborhood, not the lights in the rest of the building, just the lights in the room. The instruments were back on. Everyone laughed, applauded, and shouted, "Thank you, Lord!"

But the problem wasn't completely solved, because rooms where other activity would be going on that night were still dark. Plus, frankly, a flashlight can be a little unwieldy in the bathroom, and who wants to deal with that all evening? So Johnny walked out of the auditorium doors and blew the shofar again. Again, within three seconds the lights in the other parts of the church came on—not in the neighborhood, not in the connected buildings, but only where we needed them.[139]

Once during the worship time, in the middle of a stirring song, the power went out again. Johnny blew the shofar again. The power came back on within seconds. We had the only working lights in the neighborhood, and when the service was over, we joined the rest of the area in darkness—until Johnny stepped outside and blew again. The whole neighborhood's lights came on, and this time they stayed on. For the area beyond our neighborhood? Normal power—the kind not supplied supernaturally—was restored the next morning.

That's an example of tangible prayer, and while those of us who witnessed it don't doubt what we saw, it's still somewhat of a mystery. Why didn't Johnny just ask God to restore the power as the rest of us had been doing? God is certainly capable of hearing, responding, and glorifying his name in response to a verbal prayer. He doesn't need a trumpet blast to wake him up. So why didn't he respond to the spoken prayers of the congregation?

I don't know, and honestly I don't need to. I like the fact that God leaves us a lot of mystery to marvel at. I'm pretty sure that if the power goes out again and the shofar blows at the exact moment the service is supposed to start, there's a good chance nothing will happen. I don't think God wants to establish horn-blowing as a formula because, for one thing, we would then treat it as impersonally as flipping a light switch. And, as we've emphasized, he isn't a formula God. But he is creative, and he responds to imagination, and he loves the give and take of multidimensional and varied expression.

*I like the fact that God leaves us a lot of mystery to marvel at.*

Sometimes God responds to a verbal request, sometimes to a tangible offering, sometimes to a trumpet blast, sometimes to a prostrate position, and…well, you get the picture. Whenever we find a formula for prayer, we tend to establish a relationship with the formula and step out of fellowship with God. As long as he keeps us guessing, he keeps us in relationship. That drives systematic theologians nuts, but some of us are actually able to enjoy the adventure.

## PHYSICAL EXPRESSION

Historically, the church has fought epic battles over concrete forms of expression. One of the earliest points of contention among Christians was the use of images in worship. Was it breaking the commandment against "graven images" to depict Jesus? It was a divisive issue then, it peaked in the icon controversy between Eastern and Western churches late in the first millennium, and it is still debated by some today.[140]

But few strains of Christianity have ever opposed the idea of worship and prayer being accompanied by movement, music, water, wine, bread, and other physical expressions. The urge is planted too deeply in our psyches, and the practice is imbedded too deeply in Scripture. Prayer takes form in the physical realm.

There are two broad branches of the faith today that cultivate tangible expression to God, one traditional and the other relatively new: liturgical and charismatic. Liturgical churches spotlight symbolic architecture, the physical arrangement of sanctuaries, robes, banners, ornate crosses and furnishings, candles, sacramental elements, elaborately orchestrated music, kneeling, laying on of hands, incense (in some cases), and visual arts that depict scriptural/historical events and theological truths. Churches from a wide spectrum of denominations that have been impacted by the charismatic renewal movement spotlight dancing, shofars, banners, contemporary musical forms, shouts, multiple postures, laying on of hands, incense (in some cases), and visual arts and crafts that depict Bible stories and personal visions. In between these two streams are Protestant evangelical churches that historically reacted against some of the empty ritualism of liturgical traditions and are reluctant to exhibit informal and emotional outward expressions.

In any practice of outward display, ritualism is a risk. When we find forms of expression that are fresh and meaningful, our tendency is to repeat them so we can recapture the sense of freshness and meaning. Soon the newness is gone, and form becomes formal. What was once creative is now repetitive, and the life that was once in it seeps out until it's an empty ritual. When churches have the same expressions of worship and prayer week after week, those expressions get stale and, for most people, meaningless. That's anything but creative.

*Creative expression, like any worship or prayer, ought to always flow from the heart.*

The risk at the other end is novelty for novelty's sake. Forms of expression that are explored simply because they are antitradition are a product not so much of creativity as of restlessness. Creative expression, like any worship or prayer, ought to always flow from the heart. It should come from the heart's emotions and the Spirit's inspirations.

While most people are comfortable with some expressiveness in corporate worship and prayer, most of us rarely exhibit it in our personal time with God. A cynic would say that this is because we like showing off, and when we're alone there's no one to perform for. That's undoubtedly true of some people, but I think the main reason is that we feed off the energy of the group, and at home it's just our own lonely voice. We also convince ourselves that prayer is a matter of the heart—which is true—and that it never needs to have a concrete expression—which isn't true.

When we read of the two-way communication between God and people in the Bible, we rarely see it without some sort of tangible action involved. Our heroes of faith often communicated with God in physical ways. Abraham and Sarah washed his feet and cooked him a meal.[141] Abraham's servant traveled to the family's homeland to find a wife for Isaac and asked for a tangible sign: if the girl at the well showed compassion and selflessness by giving water not just to the servant but also to his camels, she was the God-chosen bride for Isaac.[142] Joshua and his army marched around Jericho thirteen times, blowing horns and shouting in an act of prayer and prophecy that caused the city's walls to fall.[143] Gideon prepared a meal for God and spread out some fleece as a platform for hearing God speak.[144] Naaman the Syrian had to go wash in the Jordan as an act of obedience and faith.[145] A king struck arrows against the ground, not realizing that this prophetic act was going to be interpreted as a prayer.[146] A woman broke a flask of oil over Jesus and wiped his feet with her hair.[147] Paul prayed and sang both with his spirit and with his mind.[148] The examples could go on and on.

Not only do we have these examples, we are also given instructions that, even if they aren't literal (though I think they are), at least appeal to physical images of prayer. In Psalm 98, for example, we are told to sing, shout, play lyres and trumpets, and let creation roar and clap its hands to God. Paul urged us to lift up holy hands to pray.[149] Biblical prayers involve a variety of postures, including bowing down, falling down, kneeling, waving hands, waving branches, dancing, swaying, lying down, and walking, among others.[150] They also include such actions as anointing with oil, burning incense, waving offerings, applying mud, fasting, marching, banging cymbals, blowing a shofar, raising hands, immersing in water, and sprinkling in blood. For a spiritual practice that we usually do within the confines of our heart, these are surprisingly physical gestures.

## Tangible Breath

The prophet Elisha wanted to bless a woman who had shown him generous hospitality, so he told her God would give her a child. She had been barren for years, apparently, and she didn't want to invest her heart in an empty promise. She begged the prophet not to toy with her. No, he said, it was true. She would have a son.

Elisha's words were fulfilled, and within a year the woman had a son. But one day when the boy had grown, he grabbed his head in pain and then died in his mother's lap. She laid him in Elisha's own room and then sought out the prophet. She reminded him in no uncertain terms that she had asked neither for an empty promise nor for the grief she was now experiencing.

Elisha went into the room where the boy lay and reenacted a scene from Eden. He hovered over the body—mouth to mouth, eyes to eyes, hands to hands—as if breathing into human-shaped dust. He blew the Breath of God into that lifeless form, and life returned.[151] It was a re-creation, a reminder of a genesis long ago and a foreshadowing of a more complete re-genesis to come.

Why didn't Elisha just pray? Why didn't he go into the room, say, "Lord, raise your promised son back to life," and watch the miracle happen? What compelled him to lie facedown on a body—a once-fulfilled promise that was now formless and void—and blow the Wind of God into it? It was a tangible prayer, a physical petition for God to repeat the miracle of first life. It wasn't a formula, of course; Jesus went into a room where a dead child lay, took her by the hand, and told her to arise.[152] He didn't reenact Genesis the way Elisha did, but he prayed and got the same result. So why the difference? If prayer is simply a matter of the heart, why did Elisha act it out?

*Prayer frequently involves some sort of action that has no obvious connection to the prayer.*

If we knew the answer to that, we would try to establish a pattern, develop a systematic theology of active prayer, and start to live by a principle rather than a Person. The spontaneity of our relationship with God would vanish, and in its place we'd have the predictability of a couple that has forgotten how to love and to have fun. That's not God's desire, so he leaves it mysterious. What we do know is that prayer frequently involves some sort of action, and sometimes the action has no obvious connection to the prayer.

## Spiritual Spontaneity

Late one Friday afternoon, I was at the office after almost everyone had left for the weekend. That happens frequently, as our Friday night church service is near the Walk Thru the Bible building, and there's no point in my going home during rush hour and coming back an hour later. As I was unwinding from the week, I felt an urge to anoint my hands with oil. I had a vial of myrrh and frankincense oil on my shelf—I had occasionally used it when praying for someone, but it had been a while. So I applied it to my fingertips and painted a cross on each of my palms.

When I did that, I felt a powerful electric pulse running through my arms and up and down my spine. It was an invigorating sensation, and an idea suddenly came to mind. I would go around to each of my co-workers' offices, lay my pulsating hands on their chairs, and pray for them. One of Paul's prayers seemed appropriate, so I asked God that each individual be given a spirit of wisdom and revelation, have the eyes of his or her heart enlightened, and know the hope of Jesus' calling, the riches of the glory of his inheritance, and the surpassing greatness of his power toward those who believe.[153] The entire editorial team received prayer in absentia that afternoon.

Did that do any good? Only God knows, but I have to believe the Spirit who broods and breathes over his creation wanted to touch his people that day. Could he have done that without oil? Without the energized hands of an average guy? Without a physical touch on the places where his people sit? Of course he could; he's God. He can do anything he wants. I've prayed that same prayer for my co-workers before, sans oil and touch, and I'm sure God answered. But I'll remember this prayer because it was unlike the others. I did something tangible in response to a spiritual impulse, and God did something tangible in response to me. I love it when that happens.

I know better than to expect that kind of evidence every time I pray. I could anoint my hands with oil today and feel nothing, or I could do it and experience something entirely different. God could lead me to pray for someone else, or he could shut me up in my office and do something deep in my needy heart. The point is that spiritual spontaneity, even though it makes a lot of people nervous, is desirable. God seems to enjoy variety in the way he communicates with us and we with him.

> *Spiritual spontaneity, even though it makes a lot of people nervous, is desirable.*

I have no qualms about coupling actions with my prayers, even if it might appear silly to someone else. At the gym, I've put a more-than-normal amount of weight on a bar and urgently prayed, *Lord, this expresses how desperately I want this request to be granted. I'd risk a heart attack for you to answer my prayer.* I'll give it all I've got and let the adrenaline flow—at least feeling as though I've risked a heart attack, whether or not I have. Regardless of whether I successfully lift the weight or collapse under it, I've expressed the desperation of my heart.

You can find ways to express yourself like that. Jump off a higher-than-usual diving board, for example, and say, "Lord, you know that situation we've been talking about? This is what my faith looks like to me right now. I'm going for it. Let my heart be shaped by this action." You can also try a new route to work and say, "Lord, life is confusing right now. I'm trusting you to guide me in this insignificant attempt, even if I get lost. Let that translate into trust for my bigger issues." Or you can dress in the dark colors of your circumstances as a visual expression to God, and then later in the day, as an act of faith, change into the light colors of the answer you believe is coming.[154] You'll be surprised at how clearly God interacts with you on those terms sometimes. He loves the spontaneity of diverse physical expression because he hates any hint of hollow ritualism in our relationship with him.

We see God's aversion to formula and his love for variety throughout Scripture. He spoke to Moses, for example, in a burning bush, but he never did that again with anyone else. He led the Israelites around Jericho to bring down its walls, but he led them to victory over other cities by more conventional means. He gave Hezekiah a sign that his prayer was answered by causing a shadow to go in the opposite direction of its normal course, but that's the only record we have of that phenomenon. It's as if God's expression has an infinite wardrobe, and most garments are worn only once.

That's the culture of communication into which God draws us. If we express our prayers routinely in the exact same manner— always kneeling, always talking, or always on schedule—we miss the variety that keeps us fully engaged.

Prayer is portrayed in the Bible as a full cycle. It is supposed to originate with God as he inspires us to pray according to his will, though we usually aren't conscious of the inspiration. But God often tells us what to pray for: in Isaiah, he set watchmen (interceders) on the walls and instructed them to "remind" him day and night of his agenda for Israel.[155] And the same Spirit who breathed life into creation breathes prayers into us that are too deep for words.[156] When we really connect with God at an emotional level, he births the prayers of our hearts. Only then do we return them to him.

It seems only reasonable, then, that if this creative Spirit—the One who came up with the amazing variety of sights, sounds, smells, tastes, and touch that we experience in this world—is the Spirit who inspires our prayers, then our prayers will reflect something of his variety. Immersing ourselves in his culture will lead to spontaneity in physical, concrete expression. In fitting into his environment, we'll find that we are only as limited as he is. In other words, we aren't.

## GOD'S ODDITIES

In my mind, there's not much of a difference between tangible prayer and prophetic acts—the main difference being that one is when people speak to God, and the other is when God speaks to people. But both are part of prayer in the broad sense of communication with God.

In either case, there are quite a few critics. Acting out a prayer (to God) or a prophecy (from God) has been called hocus-pocus, shamanism, voodoo, paganism, witchcraft, and many more unsavory terms by rigid religious people—all accompanied by an expression of moral outrage such as, "Where is this in the Bible?!" I read recently of some praying people who drove some small stakes in the ground to symbolize territory they were claiming for God's kingdom. The reaction by some was, to say the least, heated. The reason? "I don't see that anywhere in Scripture!"[157]

The problem is that the people who label this sort of communication as unbiblical seem not to have read the Bible. They forget the oddities of God's people as they related to him in Scripture. Take Agabus, for example. He was the guy who walked up to Paul, took the apostle's belt in his hands, wrapped himself up in it, and said, "The Holy Spirit says, 'In this way the Jews of Jerusalem will bind the owner of this belt and will hand him over to the Gentiles.'"[158] If that sort of thing happened today, most churches would accuse Agabus of witchcraft or paganism—or good old-fashioned weirdness. But apparently God thought what Agabus did was biblical enough to include in the Bible.

Other examples include the people who positioned themselves to have Peter's shadow fall on them so they could be healed[159] and the people who took handkerchiefs and aprons touched by Paul to those who were sick.[160] That type of activity today would be considered shamanism by many of our most respected religious leaders. Or consider Jacob's manipulation of the genetics of his flocks by putting carefully cut poplar, almond, and plane branches in the watering troughs so the sheep would see them before they mated.[161] The levelheaded rationalists among us would call that "witchcraft." Was Elisha was a charlatan when he tossed a bowlful of salt into Jericho's water source and purified an entire city's drinking and irrigation supply?[162] What about when he threw a branch in the river and got a lost ax head to float to the surface until it could be retrieved,[163] or when he threw some grain into a pot of poisonous stew and told people they could now eat it safely?[164]

So when someone today drives a stake in the ground to "claim" territory for God's kingdom, the charges fly: "Where's that in the Bible?" Perhaps it isn't, but that *kind* of thing certainly is, not just once or twice, but all over the place. And since we serve a God who loves variety, we wouldn't want to confine ourselves rigidly to biblical precedents anyway. That would be like expecting God to speak to us in a burning bush again and again.[165] We want to be consistent with the Bible, obviously, but we aren't contradicting Scripture when we act out what we speak to God or what he speaks to us. That isn't magic or paganism. It's expression.

It's interesting that many who label expressive prayer or prophetic acts as unbiblical have no problem accepting practices like prayer-walking or lighting a candle while one prays to symbolize the flame within. These are familiar actions, so they're relatively safe. They aren't biblical, of course—at least not in the sense of being a scriptural pattern we're told to emulate today. But they seem harmless enough, so charges of flakiness aren't often flung at them. Meanwhile, prayerful acts that are equally harmless attract extraordinary venom from segments of the Christian community. The outrage seems to come from a deeper agenda, and it looks awfully similar to the Pharisees' reactions to Jesus. There's much more spite in those accusations than a simple act like putting a stake in the ground should warrant.

*Religious rigidity and the Breath of God have a long history of conflict, as evidenced by a large number of dead prophets and a certain cross on a hill.*

But creativity frequently gets that reaction, and it always has— especially when creativity steps into the arena of faith. Religious rigidity and the Breath of God have a long history of conflict, as evidenced by a large number of dead prophets and a certain cross on a hill. It isn't enough to demonstrate for critics that creative expression in general is a biblical phenomenon; each creative expression must be justified by chapter and verse, or it's considered illegitimate at best, heretical at worst. Meanwhile, the Spirit who hovered and breathed incredible diversity into his creation invites us to reflect his glory.

How can you reflect his glory? However you want to, as long as it doesn't violate his character or his revealed purposes. When you pray, walk it out, act it out, sing it out, blast it from a ram's horn, anoint something with oil, hug a prayer cloth, lay your hands on someone, kneel, jump, build a model, dress the part—whatever. If your motives are pure, you won't offend God. Let your imagination run wild in the enormous pasture of his kingdom. Immerse yourself in his rich environment. He put his impulses into you and redeemed them for himself. Let them flow for the glory of his name. Breathe the Breath he put within you.

# Eight

# ARTISTIC PRAYER

## When Words Aren't Even Needed

I was fascinated by the whole environment. In the front of the auditorium, the worship team played and sang with energy and zeal, at times going off into a spontaneous melody—together. On the right side of the platform, an artist painted a canvas in the rhythm of the music and the colors of her heart. Over in the left corner of the room, a group of young girls were dancing hand-in-hand in a circle. Nearby, a few adults were dancing too—mostly women, but also a couple of men, and all individually according to the movements of their souls. Along the back and side walls, multicolored banners were waving; some flowed gently, while others whipped vigorously. In the aisles and between the rows of seats, some worshipers lay facedown on the floor. Others stood with hands raised and tears streaming. Some swayed gently, and others sat still in their seats. And almost everyone sang.

I had never been in a church service like that. I'd been in some that tried to manufacture spontaneity and enthusiasm, but this was different. It seemed natural, like the pulsing Breath of God was ani-mating the bodies of his people. None were pushing themselves to perform, as far as I could tell. Some looked a little strange, but then this is the human race. You'll find "strange" in every walk of life. I can handle a few oddities during corporate worship if the joy is genuine and the motives seem humble. And this seemed genuinely joyful and humble.

Depending on how narrowly one defines worship, some people might have been turned off by all the expressiveness in that church service. It defied rigid structure and predictability. I, however, thought it was beautiful. It wasn't choreographed—not by human beings, anyway—but it occurred to me that it would blend nicely into the environment of heaven. It even made me think of how God must have felt the day Eden first danced, as trees bowed in the breeze, birds sang loudly (proving conclusively that beauty doesn't depend on harmony and unison), waterfalls and streams licked the landscape, floral colors exploded on nature's canvas, and fresh aro-mas filled the air. The sensory worship I had witnessed was like nature's orchestra, only more beautiful because it was a deliberate and heartfelt offering of prayer and praise.

I can't help but think that God is pleased with such displays. The people in charge of making sure the service fits everyone's expecta-tions may not, but God's expectations aren't really defined by human traditions and forms. The psalmists encouraged spontaneous wor-ship, and numerous heroes of faith demonstrated spontaneous prayer.

We've already explored how "out of the box" God and his peo-ple have always been in their expression. And in many cases, both in Scripture and in history, those expressions have been very artistic.

## ART AND SOUL

Johann Sebastian Bach composed music with his soul—all of it. His compositions are brilliantly mathematical. The patterns and number of repetitions within them often are subtly symbolic of the title theme, with twelves representing the apostles, for example, or fives representing the wounds of Christ. But beyond the precise construction of his work, it does what music does best. It's beautiful and moving.

Bach wrote for the listening audience, but he indicated in most of his compositions that he did it with Jesus' help and for God's glory.[166]

Religious art is not unusual. Adherents of most religions dance, sculpt, sing, paint, build, dramatize stories, and act out rituals in devotion to their deities. Every culture has artistic expression that's saturated with spiritual beliefs. The impulse to create inspired art is in us, even when true knowledge of God is not.

> *Every culture has artistic expression that's saturated with spiritual beliefs.*

It has always been there in Judeo-Christian history too, but our artistic expression has most often been "horizontal" communication that tells others something about our faith. Renaissance artists, for example, depicted numerous biblical scenes that inspired them, but generally for the benefit of those who would see them. The same can be said of great composers—their music was the product of a soul spilled out for whoever would listen. Bach is perhaps one of the few examples of an artist whose work wasn't primarily horizontal. His first audience was God rather than people.

Artistic prayer—including worship, praise, and prophetic listening—is "vertical" communication. It can be musical, pictorial, motional, acted, or written, with unlimited genres within each medium. Its primary purpose isn't to communicate with other people, though others may see or hear it. Its purpose is to communicate with God, to pour out one's soul in the presence of the Creator, to express the heart's desires to the Breath who designed us to have them. Many in the church today are learning to direct their creativity upward, to God himself, but we've only just begun. We have vast territory to explore.

## ONE MOTIVE, MANY METHODS

It was an ugly exchange on the battlefield.

Joram, the king of Israel, was leading his army down to Moab to quash a rebellion. (Joram, or Jehoram, is introduced in 2 Kings 3 as the son of Ahab and Jezebel. The text says he was bad, but not quite as bad as his parents—which is like saying a category 4 hurricane isn't quite as bad as a cat-5. It's not a huge compliment.)

Somehow, Joram roped Jehoshaphat, the good king of Judah, into the adventure. But with military planning as sharp and precise as my six-year-old's skills with his suction-cup bow and arrows, Joram led the coalition through a desert on the far side of the Dead Sea—which, if you think about it, should have been avoided for its name alone. After a few days, the army ran out of water.

Good Jehoshaphat's response was to ask for a prophet to inquire of the Lord. Evil Joram's response was to blame the Lord for getting him into this mess. (It somehow eluded him that the idea to attack was his, the desert-route strategy was his, and the responsibility for bringing enough water was his.)

So Joram, a Baal-worshiper like his parents, demanded that the prophet Elisha ask God about the situation. Elisha asked Joram why he wasn't barking up the wrong altar the way he always did. Joram, ever so tactfully, insisted that the whole scheme must have been God's idea to turn them over to the enemy.

Then Elisha glared at Joram and said, in effect, "You know, pal, if Jehoshaphat weren't here, I wouldn't even give you the time of day." Then, in verse 15, he offered a rebuttal that no one in the history of the world has ever been able to counter: "Bring me a harpist."

I never actually tried that rebuttal, though I'm pretty sure it would have ended a lot of arguments between me and my sister while we were growing up. Any time she tried to boss me around, I could have just looked at her and said, "Bring me a harpist!" Yeah, that might have worked.

It certainly worked with Elisha. While the harpist played, Elisha heard from God. The Lord gave him a how-to-be-delivered-from-the-brutal-wilderness-in-one-crazy-step plan that seemed absurd on the surface and looked a lot like their own blood—blood that they should have had to spill out of their own veins, but, because God is merciful, didn't actually have to. Kind of like another plan for deliverance a few centuries later.

Not only do music and art calm the heart and prepare it to hear from God, they seem sometimes to express God's thoughts more clearly and pointedly than words can. I don't know what the harpist played when Elisha called for him on the battlefield, but apparently it aided a prayer request and an answer. The result was a word from God that fit the need exactly. Creative interaction led to a miracle.

Artistic expression for its own sake easily turns self-centered, introspective, even morbid. The philosophy that says "any art is good art" simply because it expresses what's in the soul has led to a lot of bad art. Not all of it is spiritually good, since much of it flows out of sin and its consequences: despair, lust, anger, self-hatred, meaninglessness, and other shades of darkness. The world is full of artistic expression that has no connection with the Breath that enlivened the Garden. God is not a supporter of "art at any cost."

*The world is full of artistic expression that has no connection with the Breath that enlivened the Garden.*

God is, however, a supporter of artistic expression created for his glory, especially when he's the primary audience. The gate into his kind of creativity is as narrow as a single Savior, but once we're inside the kingdom, the opportunities are limitless. We are free to glorify God with whatever capacity he's given us to do so.

Even so, we question just how much freedom we have. In the early stages of his career, Mozart felt compelled to stick to established forms of music—"to imitate traditional models without transcending them."[167] He was a musical genius, regardless of style, but because of antimodernist values under which he was raised, he apparently felt the tension between meeting expectations and unleashing his imagination. One biographer calls it "an anxiety of originality."[168] Some years later, his creativity broke through the layer of conventionality, and he stretched musical forms beyond the norms of the age. Faced with the prospect of a routine career, he learned to see himself as a creator rather than an imitator.[169] Like Mozart, we explore new horizons hesitantly. For those of us who are keenly aware of being in the presence of God, this hesitation is greatly magnified. We don't want to offend the Holy One.

This tension between convention and originality is always there when we yearn to express ourselves. We are told, after all, to be imitators of God.[170] That narrows our possibilities because God isn't an "anything goes" kind of God. But then we learn that the God we are to imitate is wildly expressive, and our possibilities broaden again. We don't want to violate his character, but we also don't want to place ungodly limits on ourselves. We hang in the balance between method and meaning, where God-ordained meaning is clearly defined, and God-ordained method is a wide-open field. We often get caught in the tension.

And the stakes are high. In Scripture, we see vertical artistry applied two ways: in the crafting of idols, and in the crafting of articles of true worship. One is to be avoided like the plagues that result from it; the other is to be pursued with a passion. Creative expression is like fire. It's indispensable for warming homes and cooking food, but it can also cloud the skies or consume a forest. Misusing it can have devastating consequences.

Artistic prayer brings the wildness of creativity under the authority of God while raising it above the limits of verbiage. But we have to be careful with it. When artistry honors the created and ignores the Creator, it isn't worthwhile. When we engage in vertical expression, motive is everything. We have to guard ours zealously.

> *Artistic prayer brings the wildness*
> *of creativity under the authority*
> *of God while raising it above*
> *the limits of verbiage.*

We see the perfect example of this tension between Godward expression and impure motives when King David brought the ark of the covenant into Jerusalem. As this Spirit-breathed work of art approached the city, David began to leap and dance in gratitude and praise. The text says his wild display was "before the LORD." That's not how his wife saw it, though. From her perspective, he was foolish and undignified (and partly undressed) before the servant girls, as though he was trying to impress them. And she "despised him in her heart."[171]

This is exactly the dynamic we see in expressive worship today. What one person does with a pure motive is judged by an onlooker who assumes an impure motive. What feels like worship to some looks like foolishness to others. The expressiveness of the human soul often makes sense only to the one expressing it. And motive, which is seen clearly by God, remains invisible.

It's true that the creative expression of some flows from motives of pride and performance. But it's also true that the creative expression of others flows from grateful, worshipful hearts. On the outside, the two may look exactly the same. If David had, in fact, been dancing for the sake of the young ladies present, his wife would have been right to rebuke him. But his dance wouldn't have looked any different. The only variable was his motive, which means that the point at which these expressions differed was hidden from human eyes. What we have to keep in mind when we express ourselves to God artistically is that only one opinion matters: his. And his comes from what he alone can see in our hearts.

A fear of how we will be perceived inhibits many of us from being imaginative. We don't want to give the wrong impression—that we're showing off, or that we have no idea how foolish we appear, or that we think we're talented when we're not, or that we think we can impress God by our originality. But those thoughts are based on the idea that God cares about how others perceive us when we worship, and that idea is found nowhere in Scripture. If God's reaction to Michal's judgment of David's undignified dance is any indication, he isn't the least bit impressed when we choose respectability over heartfelt worship. She thought David was being a disruptive show-off. She didn't see how his reckless expressiveness could possibly glorify the Lord. The Lord, however, did. And only one opinion counted.

## FEARLESS CREATIVITY

Even if we see how our creativity can glorify God, we often lack confidence in our ability to express it well. I've heard—and told myself—this common excuse: "My talents aren't good enough to capture my prayers." No offense intended to those with the gift of gab, but neither are our words. Paul made that clear in Romans 8:26–27, when he wrote that the Spirit has to help us in our weakness by expressing our prayers in groans too deep for words. The assumption that our words are more adequate than our creative forms of communication comes from our ease with spoken language and our insecurity about undeveloped talents. It doesn't come from Scripture.

> *Prayer goes deeper
> than both words and art.*

Artistic prayer isn't going to change the fact that the Breath of God groans through us and on our behalf. Prayer goes deeper than both words and art. The Spirit still needs to take what we offer and translate it for his purposes and our good. But we're much more engaged in the prayer process when we can spill some of our own deep groanings out on paper, in song, or in movement.

For some reason, our insecurities about our talents grips us much more tightly than insecurities in other areas. Most of us aren't afraid to cook a quick meal, draft a business proposal, or compete on a field—at least, not compared with painting a canvas, writing a song, or sculpting clay. Perhaps that's because our creativity is so much more personal. It comes from the depths of our souls, and that's just how far rejection would penetrate. So we're afraid to step out and make something that God will certainly see or hear, and others might as well. It feels the same as standing naked before a crowd.

We need to remember the audience of One—the audience that David danced for and that Bach composed for. Prayer in all its forms should be wholly concerned with God's opinion and not with anyone else's. Presenting God with something the critics would like is not the goal.

The first time I sang a spontaneous prayer to God, for example, anyone who heard it would have laughed. I sounded like a soloist who forgot the words *and* the melody in the middle of the song and was desperately trying to recover. But I don't think God was going to be impressed with the smooth stylings of this singer anyway. Regardless of what came out, it wouldn't measure up to the inexpressible beauty of heaven's music. We can't tickle God's ears because he doesn't have ears like ours. To him, beautiful music is defined by its source. If we have the right motives and are vulnerable before him, it sounds great.

Surely we can understand that. The young man who expresses his devotion to his sweetheart with a gift that took days for him to make probably isn't going to be judged for the quality of his work.

(If he is, he needs to forget about her and move on.) His beloved will look past his feeble attempt and see the devotion that went into it, and she'll treasure it as the act of love that it is. The child who spends all morning making a construction-paper flower for her mommy is going to get major hugs, even if Mommy has to ask what it's supposed to be. That's because the heart's devotion isn't measured by talent and skill. It's measured by motive.

## All for You

In the 1998 film adaptation of *Great Expectations*—the Dickens novel recast in a modern setting—the main character, artist Finnegan Bell, explodes with emotion after his first gallery exhibit. On the street outside the apartment of Estella, a childhood friend who plays with the hearts of men before destroying them and who is now engaged to a successful businessman, a desperate Finnegan pours out his soul.

"Don't you understand that everything I do, I do it for you?" he screams to an empty window above him. "Anything that might be special in me is you!"

She was his muse, his inspiration, buried deep within him secretly for years. In spite of her rejection, and in spite of his insistence that he'd long forgotten her, she was the one who stirred his creativity.

*We have the ultimate Muse.*

We have the ultimate Muse. Anything that is special in us is him. In spite of our casual prayers, in spite of our misconceptions about the depth of his love, he is the One who stirs our creativity.

Love makes the heart beat faster and stretches the soul to express itself in imaginative ways. It needs many, many outlets.

Have you ever danced your passions before God like David did? Your movements can often express your heart much better than your words. Embarrassment is completely unnecessary—remember your singular Audience—but since it so often accompanies this activity, especially at first, try it when you're alone. No angels will laugh, and like a parent who enjoys seeing the heart of an expressive child, God will appreciate the effort. He made your body to move like it does, and he even commanded you to dance.[172] His people danced without rebuke frequently in Scripture.[173] This isn't exactly a novel concept.

But for many people it seems to be, and dancing can be a little unnerving. In the realm of free artistic expression, charismatics major on the "free," liturgicals major on the "artistic," and everyone else is a little wary of both. Dance is one of the more suspicious expressions to God. We need to remember that it has a long history of acceptance in biblical and Hebrew culture and in the early church. If God didn't like it, it seems as if he would have said so sometime before the late medieval era, when the church began to frown on it.[174]

But maybe you've tried dancing your prayers and worship to God, and it just isn't making the connection for you. How about drawing the mood of your soul, with all its worries and fears? Or sketching your artistic interpretation of the obstacles in the way of your calling? Or even drawing your desires? That's what my son Timothy does for me. Sure, he could just tell me that his Christmas wish is the black remote-control car with flames on the side, all-terrain traction and suspension, hidden antenna, removable hood and doors, and spring-cushioned bumpers. But his detailed drawings in living color reveal so much more about how deeply this wish smolders in his heart. (He also generously provides the catalog's item number for the linear-thinking side of my brain.) Somehow, the care and enthusiasm he puts into his drawing affects me much more than a descriptive request would.

Maybe you like to sing your prayers and praises. Many people do and are quite comfortable doing so. Nearly all churches of all eras have freely used the human voice in worship and prayer. But what about in your private time with God? Have you ever spontaneously sung your requests to God or made up a tune that expresses your heart toward him? As with dance and drawing, it doesn't matter if you think it sounds good. The audience of One will love it.

Or maybe you play an instrument. You can play for him a tune you already know, if it expresses the prayer in your heart, or you can make up something entirely new. How do you play a musical prayer? If you're struggling with the trials of life and need God to lift you up, start with a low and tumultuous tune. Then gradually raise it, smooth it out, and let it end up joyful and victorious, or calm and peaceful. In your heart, you're expressing to God where you are now and where you're asking him to take you. The only difference is that your thoughts are coming out in melodies rather than words. If you want victory, play victoriously. If you want peace, play peacefully. If you want someone to change, make a melody that reflects that change. At times, you'll be amazed at how the Breath of God flows through your instrument. You'll also usually find your spiritual atmosphere changing dramatically.

Many people write their prayers in a journal. That can be as uncreative as writing an instruction manual, but it doesn't have to be.

Why not write a short story with yourself as the main character? Have it express your current situation and turn the plot in the direction of the desire you are presenting to God. Or write a personality profile of yourself, and ask God how he would rewrite it. Then let him inspire a new image for you to write about.

When you can, write in metaphors that capture the images that inspire you—or that trouble you. This is how David wrote his psalms. His physical battles, hiding in caves, being surrounded by enemies, and so on, came out in the psalms as rich spiritual symbols. Today, for example, we hardly know what a tower of refuge is, but the metaphor means something to us because of how David used it.[175] Most of us haven't ever seen a deer panting for water, but we hold the picture in our minds because of how David wrote his prayer to God.[176] When you write your prayers, use pictures and sounds and smells to describe your thoughts and requests. The fullness of your expression will stick in your memory, shape your faith, and fuel your prayers again in the following days as the scene develops in your mind.

Take it a step further, if you like, and write something poetic. I've heard it said that while many people like to write poetry, few like to read it. God does, however. He inspired quite a bit of it in his Word, and much of it was directed specifically to him. His people, filled with his Breath, have poured out their guts in rhyme, rhythm, and images because those things sometimes express the heart better than prose. Biblical poetry is full of anguish, hope, anger, delight, doubt, faith, and more. For psalmists and prophets, it was often God's preferred medium of communication.

> *Biblical poetry is full of anguish, hope, anger, delight, doubt, faith, and more.*

A woman who sometimes comes to our church expresses herself to God in sign language. She doesn't have to, as neither she nor God has any trouble hearing. And she undoubtedly has many other ways of communicating her prayers and praise as well. But when she signs along with the music, she's as expressive as a ballerina. Something happens in the spiritual atmosphere when her hands start dancing to the rhythm of worship. Most of us don't know exactly what those hands are saying, but God does. And even for the rest of us, they communicate beyond words. It's like eavesdropping on a sacred conversation and knowing the Listener is present.

We could go on and on with artistic outlets for prayer, but you get the idea. It's possible to express the thoughts, desires, praises, doubts, fears, faith, and love of the heart in plenty of wordless languages. I've seen canvases, clay, video screens, banners, notebook paper, and choreography that speak volumes to the Creator. And I've heard instruments, choirs, bands, chants, and drums that do the same. Nowhere in Scripture are we told that prayer equals words. It often includes them—usually, in fact—but certainly not always. The point is to somehow communicate our inner heart to the listening Lord. As the Author of artistry, he understands the language.

"A composer has discovered within himself shaping powers, imaginative powers, the power to visualize a musical structure before creating it in reality, the power to transmute inner feelings into objective forms," wrote a biographer of Mozart. "As wish, his music tells of the landscapes he wants to inhabit.... As memory, his music tells of what he has experienced. As desire, his music tells of what he wants to enfold in his arms."[177] As prayer, we might add, our artistry tells of the deepest longings we want our Father to touch with his power and love.

Artistic prayer is important because prayer expresses the movements of a person's spirit, and the spirit can't be contained in one or two modes of expression. It's part of our process of fitting into the environment of heaven. While anyone can create art from deep within, only someone reborn by the Breath of God can fully breathe his artistry back to him. Only his Spirit can inspire prayers that touch his heart with expressions too deep for words.

# Nine

# INTIMATE PRAYER

## The Love Language of God

Male seahorses are my heroes, and the females are my role models. Why? Because in the world of the *Hippocampus*— that's the scientific name for a seahorse, if you want to throw it around to impress people—it's the men who give birth. He's the stable one in whom the little sea filly deposits her eggs. Inside his pouch, he fertilizes them and incubates them. Then he gives birth to hundreds at a time.

This provides a great rebuttal to every woman who says, "I wish you men could be pregnant so you know what it feels like!" We men can respond with the facts: "Hey, our seahorse brothers do enough of that for the rest of us."

But even more than a good retort, the mating life of seahorses is one of God's visual illustrations of creative prayer. The courtship leading up to the mating act demonstrates how expressive creatures can be when they want to get intimate.

The seven-month breeding season begins with the male and female meeting regularly each morning. She can always find him in the same place, anchored to a blade of grass in the seabed. Having spent the time since their last meeting roaming over wide territory, encountering and ignoring numerous other males along the way, she arrives for her morning visit—the same male, the same time each day. This is the get-to-know-each-other stage, as there's no actual mating yet, but they're already committed. She only has eyes for him, and their faithfulness continues throughout the breeding season and beyond.

During their morning visit, male and female seahorses dance. They wrap their tails together and float in and out of the sea grass, sometimes twirling and sometimes changing their colors for each other. This expressive ritual establishes their sense of unity and commitment. Only then, when their long-term relationship has been established, does the male open up his pouch and invite the female to deposit her eggs. And they remain strictly faithful to each other because they've taken the time to bond.[178]

Not only is seahorse courtship creative in the sense of being imaginative and colorful; it's also creative in producing tiny new seahorses. The bond of intimacy the male and female establish with each other becomes the environment both for self-expression and for new life.

I began by saying that male seahorses were my heroes. That's because they do for their children what God does for us. He's the anchor in turbulent waters, the fertilizer, the incubator, and the nurturer.

But the females are my role models. That's because for all their roaming around the seahorse world—they frequently get caught up in the turbulent waters while the male is wrapped securely around sea grass—they know who they're committed to. They come back to the same male every morning and dance with him. And then after days of mutual bonding, they offer up their eggs in the same way we offer up our prayers. "Here, Lord. Take them, fertilize them, incubate them, birth them." And then the process starts all over again, almost immediately.

## EXPRESSIVE LOVE

The 1998 Oscar-winning film *Shakespeare in Love* opens with Will Shakespeare working on a play for which he has no inspiration. "It's all locked safe in here," he tells his patron, pointing to his own head. "As soon as I find my muse."

This response, of course, is somewhat alarming to Henslowe, the patron who has commissioned him. He knows what it means: Will hasn't started writing yet, though the script is due in two weeks. Henslowe wants answers.

"Henslowe, you have no soul," Will tells him, "so how can you understand the emptiness that seeks a soul mate?"

Later in a session with a "doctor" who seems to be a cross between a psychologist and a fortune-teller, Will pours out his heart. "Words, words, words. Once, I had the gift. I could make love out of words as a potter makes cups out of clay, love that overthrows empires, love that binds two hearts together come hellfire and brimstones. For sixpence a line, I could cause a riot in a nunnery."

But now it has all changed. "I have lost my gift," he says. "It's as if my quill is broken, as if the organ of the imagination has dried up, as if the proud tower of my genius has collapsed."

Will finds his muse, of course, in the person of Viola, a well-to-do girl who wants to be on stage in an era when even female parts were played by men. He falls in love with her, and the words start flowing. The comedy *Romeo and Ethel* turns into the tragedy *Romeo and Juliet*—his feelings breathe life into Romeo, hers into Juliet—and a masterpiece is born. Love spawns a rush of creativity.

That's the way it is with us. Most of the world's greatest, most profuse expression has come from the fertile environment of romantic love. History's most famous songs, novels, and poems have been, more often than not, written because somebody fell in love with somebody else—or was devastated when love didn't work out. This romantic impulse is so deeply planted within us that it generates our strongest passions and greatest imaginations. When we love, we pursue our beloved as creatively as we know how. And when we bond with our beloved, we create new life together.

> *When we bond with our beloved,*
> *we create new life together.*

How does that happen? A man broods over his wife, hovering and breathing and implanting seeds into her—just as the Breath hovered over the waters and breathed life into Adam's dust, just as Elisha hovered over a boy and breathed new life into his dead body, just as the Breath of Ezekiel's prophecy resurrected dry bones, just as the Spirit of Genesis overshadowed Mary and fertilized a Savior within her womb, just as Jesus got face-to-face with the disciples and breathed the Holy Spirit into them, just as this Breath of God broods over us and births us anew.

The Spirit of the re-genesis is illustrated again and again in Scripture, and the climax of all illustrations is perhaps Paul's metaphor of marriage. When a man and a woman leave their mothers and fathers and become one flesh, it's a picture of something far greater, he said. "This mystery is profound, and I am saying that it refers to Christ and the church."[179] We forsake the worldly culture that nurtured us and become one with Christ—his very own body, flesh and Spirit joined together—to live as new creatures. With each of us, God does what he did with the dust of Eden: he breathes the Breath of life into us, and we rise in oneness with him. It doesn't get any more creative than that. Intimacy is how babies—physical and spiritual—are made.

## THE IMAGE OF GOD

The Bible gives us plenty of images portraying God's relationship with redeemed humanity. He is as a master is to a servant, as a gardener is to a vineyard, as a potter is to clay, as a father is to a child, or as a mother is to a baby.

The most profound and enduring image, however, is as bridegroom to a bride. Rabbinic literature throughout the ages has described the Ten Commandments and the Sinai covenant as a marriage contract and ceremony. Solomon's Song has long been interpreted by rabbis as an allegory of God's love for Israel, and pastors have long interpreted it as an allegory of Christ's love for the church. The last book of Scripture ends with the wedding to end all weddings. This is not a newfangled representation of God.

Jesus spoke parables of the Bridegroom returning for his bride, and he gave his disciples that very picture when he told them, "In My Father's house are many dwelling places.... If I go and prepare a place for you, I will come again and receive you to Myself, that where I am, there you may be also."[180] This is much like what a man might tell his prospective bride after an engagement contract. When the home was prepared, he would return with his friends, blowing a shofar to signal his arrival. When Scripture tells us Jesus will return at the sound of a trumpet, and all the angels with him, this is what it means. It's time for the wedding.

*The relentless urge that drives us to pursue our passions is nothing to be ashamed of.*

No wonder God's gift of intimate physical relationships is so wild and powerful. I tell men that the raging river within them—that relentless urge that drives us to pursue our passions—is nothing to be ashamed of. It attracts plenty of pointed fingers accusing it of depravity, but if God meant it to represent the passion with which he created the world and the zeal with which the Bridegroom comes to redeem it, it *has* to be nearly untamable. It's our job to channel that river in the right direction, of course, and we must if we are to portray the Bridegroom well. But to say it's by nature sinful? Never. The drive to hover and breathe and impart seeds of life was there at the foundation of the world. We have to embrace it.

Women, too, yearn to embrace it, especially when men realize what this passion represents and guard it in sacred stewardship. The deep desire of a woman to be loved and wanted is also, like a man's drive, nothing to be ashamed of. It's a picture of the human race opening up to the Breath of God, inviting his creative expressions of love and intimacy, and offering our fertility for his breeding. The creativity in Eden, reflected throughout Scripture and in romance and marriage, is a portrait of intimacy between God and those made in his image. That's why Scripture begins with a brooding Spirit and ends with a magnificent wedding banquet. That's why Jesus' first recorded miracle was at a marriage feast. And that's why the act of sex is absolutely sacred. It's a powerful and perfect illustration of the ways God expresses himself to us, and we to him.

## A SACRED IMAGE IN A CORRUPT CULTURE

When I started this chapter, I almost felt that I should preface it with a warning: "Due to the graphic nature of the following discussion, reader discretion is advised." That's because the enemy has gone all out in his efforts to corrupt, twist, distort, and pollute the picture of God's passionate love. If this picture of intimacy illustrates the emotions God had when he created the world, redeemed the world, pursued us and saved us, and comes again for the consummation of love, it's a picture that makes Satan bristle. The pursuit of sexual intimacy is where human beings rise to their highest levels of creativity, and the act of sexual intimacy is where God raises us to procreativity. This kind of intimacy is a fertile field that grows new expressions and new life. It embodies the intensity of God's love, so corrupting it is at the top of Satan's strategic initiatives. He has done everything he can do to defile this image—fertility cults, pornography, immoral relationships outside marriage, rape, incest, homosexuality, pedophilia, and on and on and on. He's a vandal who's hellbent on defacing the masterpiece.

*We have a hard time conceiving of sexuality as completely pure and an even harder time applying that image to God.*

Because he has been so successful at profaning the sacred image of divine intimacy, many people are extremely uncomfortable with the idea of our relationship with God having sexual undertones. We have a hard time conceiving of sexuality as completely pure and an even harder time applying that image to God. It seems scandalous to us, rife with gross impurities, distortions, and hints of pagan fertility rites. So to even mention intimacy with God in these terms is controversial.

But the Bible frequently uses terms of courtship and romantic love to portray God's passion. We've already discussed many of them: At Sinai, he made a marriage contract with his chosen people. In the Song of Solomon, he's the Lover captivated by his beloved. In the Prophets, he's a jilted husband lamenting the unfaithfulness of his precious wife.[181] In Jesus' parables, he's the beaming Father of a very eager Bridegroom. And in Revelation, the Bridegroom finally delights in the ultimate embrace. These undertones, however scandalous they may seem, are thoroughly biblical.

Using this image of intimacy, then, is not an attempt to sexualize God. Rather, God sexualized us because we were made in his likeness. We were designed as male and female to represent his courtship of humanity and the eventual consummation of his love. Physical intimacy may have connotations of corruption in our minds, but it shouldn't in this context. God has never had an impure thought. An intimate relationship with him is not scandalous, it's sacred.

## "KNOWING" GOD

Because of the nature of our relationship with God, prayer must go beyond words. Intimacy is more than a matter of saying the right things and passing along the right information. From seahorses to sweethearts, it begins with the dance of courtship, and only gets more creative after that. Like the young man in this book's introduction,

God pours out his imaginative expression in an effort to win our hearts. Unless we respond—creatively, seductively, intimately—our relationship with him falls short of his glory.

Historically, many Christians have seen the Lord's Supper as a wedding feast. This is creative communion, a physical representation of deeper intimacy with Jesus. It's a theme that has been echoed repeatedly throughout the church's past, especially among hermits and mystics.[182] While many speak to God as Creator, Master, and Father—all appropriate and biblical—others speak to him as the Lover of their souls. When we grasp the intimate nature of our relationship with God, our prayers begin to sound different—like the familiar and personal conversations of a couple in love.

One of Scripture's most moving illustrations of the creative nature of intimate prayer is the story of Ruth. The young widow could have had Naomi approach their kinsman Boaz to suggest a marriage proposal. Or she could have approached him herself, explaining that according to God's Law, she needed to marry a kinsman, and he seemed to be a likely candidate, if he'd be kind enough to consider it. But that's a transaction, not a romance. Love doesn't work that way; it's much more creative.

So Ruth, with Naomi's helpful guidance, prepared herself by bathing and applying oils and perfumes to herself. Then she waited until nighttime, after Boaz had been working all day in the fields and eating and drinking all evening with the guys. When Boaz was sound asleep, she "came softly and uncovered his feet and lay down."[183] She just lay there, spread before him—modestly, yes, but provocatively too—and let her visual suggestion speak louder than words. "Spread your wings over your servant," she said enticingly, inviting him into her drama, "for you are a redeemer."[184]

Boaz was impressed that this proper young woman boldly

pursued an older man, without regard to wealth or other prospects. She did not whisper a secret desire or a face-saving hint. Though a proposal of words might have accomplished an engagement, this suggestive picture—a pretty woman, the smells of perfume, the secrecy of the night, a risky venue where other men lay—won his heart. For Boaz, what earlier was subtle interest transformed into a heart-pounding, romantic bond, all because Ruth spoke the graphic language of love.

*Creativity of expression developed into creativity from expression.*

This picturesque courtship, dramatic and daring, led to a line of progeny that included King David and the Messiah. Creativity *of* expression developed into creativity *from* expression. That's a beautiful portrait of prayer.

In the end, that's what our prayers are meant to accomplish—creation. God gives us creative roles: Adam in assigning names and identities to the animals, Adam and Eve in being fruitful and multiplying. And he gives us roles in the new creation: naming, praying for, working out his agenda, binding and loosing, healing and delivering, sharing his love, and imparting his Spirit. He's generating the kingdom of God, and our prayers are powerful procreative acts. We, too, are to be fruitful and multiply. If we want people to be born of his Spirit, if we want to bear the fruit of the Spirit ourselves—in other words, if we want to experience the fertility of his kingdom—we have to understand the place of intimacy where his love breeds. We have to commune with the Breath of God as he hovers and broods and exhales in our faces and imparts his seed into our innermost being with unrelenting passion and sweet tenderness.

Only then will life unfold and the new creation spring up. Intimacy, as we've noted, is how babies—physical and spiritual—are conceived.

To get to that place of intimacy, we would do well to follow Ruth's example and approach our Redeemer with the graphic language of love—sweet-smelling oils, suggestive whispers, daring venues, gracious words, acts of devotion, whatever it takes. Creativity has no shortage of options. If we love him enough, we'll pursue ways to commune with him that bring forth life. Love *always* finds expression.

## A Man in Labor

Because of the wickedness of King Ahab and his wife, Jezebel, the prophet Elijah declared a drought in the name of the Lord. It seemed reasonable, as people desperate for food often turn back to God. So Israel endured famine for three years.

Near the end of the time of drought, Elijah challenged the priests of Baal to a spiritual duel at Mount Carmel. Eight hundred and fifty pagan worshipers showed up to demonstrate the power of their false gods. Elijah, alone in his opposition, suggested that two altars be built; whichever caught on fire supernaturally would point to the true God. The altar to Baal, of course, did not catch fire. Elijah's altar to God, though daringly drenched in water, did. And all the people began to worship the true God.

Elijah told Ahab to go eat and drink, since the people had turned their hearts, and the drought would soon be over. Then he did a strange thing. He went to the top of the mountain and prayed for rain. But he didn't just utter a prayer; he squatted down and put his face between his knees. Why? No one knows for sure, but the position he took was the same position in which women of many cultures, probably including ancient Israel's, give birth. Elijah apparently didn't just pray. He *labored* in prayer, as if he were delivering a baby.

Elijah sent his servant several times to check the skies, because he knew that a prayer from the place of intimacy bears fruit. And this one was no exception. A small cloud soon turned into a large cloud, and rain poured. The drought was over. God had answered.[185]

The ultimate purpose of prayer is to bring the bride of Christ into a deeper love relationship with him, and that deeper love eventually results in the labor of childbirth. The incarnation of Christ even began this way, with the Breath of God hovering over Mary—overshadowing her, it says[186]—and breathing life into the womb that would bear the second Adam, as he had done in Eden with the first Adam.[187]

*We present our needs and desires creatively, passionately, and intimately, and he brings forth fruit.*

We can assume that because God does nothing halfway, this kind of intimacy in prayer can be accurately illustrated in the most extreme terms of human love. We offer ourselves to God, and he impregnates us with his purposes and his promises. We nurture this kingdom growth by presenting to him the needs and desires that rise out of our union with him. We present them creatively, passionately, and intimately, and he brings forth fruit. The process of prayer itself may be intangible, but the expression isn't. And it can be emotionally overwhelming.

Perhaps this is why barrenness was the consequence of Michal's scorn when she rebuked David for his undignified dance. You miss out on the vitality of an intimate relationship when you think it looks foolish. When you hold creative passion in contempt, you can't participate in its fruitfulness.

## Be the Beloved

Read the Song of Solomon sometime through a lens that sees it as a prayer model. Imagine it as a description of intimate communion between you and God. What senses does the beloved bring into the conversation? What images does she invoke? Is she conversing with an acquaintance? Does she sound as if she's talking on the phone? Read these excerpts and see:

*Beloved*:

Listen! My beloved!
Behold, he is coming,
Climbing on the mountains,
Leaping on the hills!
My beloved is like a gazelle or a young stag.
Behold, he is standing behind our wall,
He is looking through the windows,
He is peering through the lattice.

My beloved responded and said to me,
"Arise, my darling, my beautiful one,
And come along.
For behold, the winter is past,
The rain is over and gone.
The flowers have already appeared in the land;
The time has arrived for pruning the vines,

And the voice of the turtledove has been heard in our land.
The fig tree has ripened its figs,
And the vines in blossom have given forth their fragrance.
Arise, my darling, my beautiful one,
And come along!"

*Lover*:

O my dove, in the clefts of the rock,
In the secret place of the steep pathway,
Let me see your form,
Let me hear your voice;
For your voice is sweet,
And your form is lovely.
Catch the foxes for us,
The little foxes that are ruining the vineyards,
While our vineyards are in blossom.

*Beloved*:

My beloved is mine, and I am his;
He pastures his flock among the lilies.
Until the cool of the day when the shadows flee away,
Turn, my beloved, and be like a gazelle
Or a young stag on the mountains of Bether.

On my bed night after night I sought him
Whom my soul loves;
I sought him but did not find him.
"I must arise now and go about the city;

In the streets and in the squares
I must seek him whom my soul loves."
I sought him but did not find him.
The watchmen who make the rounds in the city found me,
And I said, "Have you seen him whom my soul loves?"
Scarcely had I left them
When I found him whom my soul loves;
I held on to him and would not let him go
Until I had brought him to my mother's house,
And into the room of her who conceived me....

*Beloved*:

I was asleep but my heart was awake.
A voice! My beloved was knocking:
"Open to me, my sister, my darling,
My dove, my perfect one!
For my head is drenched with dew,
My locks with the damp of the night."
I have taken off my dress,
How can I put it on again?
I have washed my feet,
How can I dirty them again?
My beloved extended his hand through the opening,
And my feelings were aroused for him.
I arose to open to my beloved;
And my hands dripped with myrrh,
And my fingers with liquid myrrh,
On the handles of the bolt.
I opened to my beloved,

But my beloved had turned away and had gone!
My heart went out to him as he spoke.
I searched for him but I did not find him;
I called him but he did not answer me.
The watchmen who make the rounds in the city found me,
They struck me and wounded me;
The guardsmen of the walls took away my shawl from me.
I adjure you, O daughters of Jerusalem,
If you find my beloved,
As to what you will tell him:
For I am lovesick.[188]

According to ancient rabbinic and historical Christian interpretations, the Song is an allegory of God and his beloved. Therefore, the words just quoted represent words God's people speak to him. They are intimate, intense, playful, sensory, sensual, and full of creativity. Though we may blush at them, they profess appropriate sentiments in our expression to God.

Prayer, ultimately, is about intimate love. When we're in love with a human being, we get remarkably creative. So when we're not very creative in our expressions to God, what does that say about our love?

Perhaps it says that we are like the beloved in the introductory parable in this book, the woman who spoke only words to the man who showered her with expressions of love. If that's the case, try quoting the above excerpts of the Song to your Savior. Try asking him to work his way intimately into your heart. Cultivate the language of intimacy because this is the language of the kingdom. This is where transformation occurs, where we become "one flesh" and one heart with God. This is where the new creation is born.

# Ten

# FULL-CONTACT PRAYER

## A Sacred Lifestyle

M ake my life a prayer to you."

That line comes from a song Keith Green sang, and it captures the fullness of biblical prayer.[189] When Paul told the Romans to present their bodies to God as a living sacrifice, he probably assumed that prayer would be part of the presentation. Our communication with God is to be well-rounded.

In Scripture, as we have seen, prayer is like a full-contact sport. It reflects the creativity of the Breath of God and involves our intellects, emotions, and bodies. It's a holistic enterprise that intimately connects everything in us with God himself. It flows out of the great commandment given to Israel and reiterated by Jesus: "You shall love the Lord your God with all your heart, and with all your soul, and with all your mind, and with all your strength."[190] Though this commandment isn't specifically about prayer—indeed, it's comprehensive enough to include all of life—expressing ourselves to God is certainly included in this relationship of love.

In the Bible, people often communicated with God in meals, as with Abraham's hospitality, the Passover remembrance, the other feasts of Israel, and the Lord's Supper. When they prepared their hearts each year for the time of the Passover, they cleansed their houses of every speck of leaven as a physical expression of an inner purging. When they repented, they spoke to God and others by dressing in sackcloth and covering themselves with ashes. When they asked God to cleanse them, they immersed themselves in a baptismal bath. When they expressed their grief to God and others, they tore their clothes. When a servant wanted to remain committed to the family he served, he would pierce his ear as a statement to God and others. When God's people communicated with him through sacrificial offerings, they were extremely careful about the kinds of animals they offered; and when they burned incense in their worship, they used a precise mixture designated by God.[191]

Why was God so particular about issues like the quality of animal sacrifices and the recipe for incense? Because these things weren't random; each made a specific statement. They expressed spiritual truths in physical pictures.[192] The point is that, historically and biblically, communication between God and humanity has usually been a full sensory experience.

*Historically and biblically, communication between God and humanity has usually been a full sensory experience.*

In our age, we've lost some of the comprehensive nature of our prayers. We don't tear our clothes anymore to express our grief, we don't cover ourselves in ashes when we repent, we often go through communion as a mere ritual, we get embarrassed to think of God with the intensity of a romantic relationship, we write checks rather than offer our possessions, we have few or no criteria for the candles we burn in worship and prayer because any flame will do, and on and on. It isn't that God has given us detailed instructions for expression that we've failed to follow. He has wide parameters for prayers. The issue is more a matter of our approach to him. When we make prayer a completely inward, private matter, it can easily get lost amid the clutter of our hearts.

We do have some ways of visibly expressing our conversations with him, however, and we can use those as a starting point. We sing, of course, and we bow our heads or kneel. Those are probably the most common unspoken forms of communication we use. But we also frequently express ourselves in symbols, like being baptized (at its deepest level, a prayer for resurrection life), rubbing ashes on our forehead at the beginning of Lent, swinging censers (in Orthodox and a few other worship services), lighting candles, raising hands, dancing, and more. These are generally corporate acts of vertical communication, and they help us connect with God.

But for most of us, there remains an enormous gap between what we do in public worship and what we do in private. Why is that? The audience hasn't changed. We still have an audience of One. Granted, some expressions like choral music and processions are group efforts, but many are not. Many are just as valid in private as in public—even more so, one might argue, because there's no unconscious urge to perform for others when we act alone. There's only us and God, and nothing to prove to anyone else.

That's why creative prayer—imaginative, emotional, tangible, artistic, and intimate—makes our relationship with God more real. It becomes concrete in the context of the prayer closet and creates an environment of two-way communication that otherwise eludes us. When we pray to God only inwardly and silently, we subconsciously expect him to speak to us only inwardly and silently. Our narrow focus in praying also narrows our focus in hearing. Like a couple who speaks by phone occasionally, we miss out on the full range of relationship.

*The eternal Word became dusty flesh and dwelt among us.*

When we pray creatively, with all our senses and circumstances, a strange thing happens to our approach to life. The lines that once divided us into two compartments, the secular and the sacred, begin to blur. We begin to see everything around us as sacred. The mundane elements of our world become potential articles of heaven, prime candidates to pick up and use as the language of God. That sacred/secular divide that God once seemed so reluctant to bridge—that gap that made us feel so disconnected from the One who made us, redeemed us, and left us in a very physical world—is now bridged by the elements of earth, similar to the day the eternal Word became dusty flesh and dwelt among us. The divide was conquered then, and it's conquered every time we take what is common and use it sacredly. We tangibly connect with God, and life becomes rich and full.

## PRACTICALLY CREATIVE

If you find yourself wondering how, practically, to make your relationship with God a richer and fuller experience, the following are some ideas to get you started.

### Sight

- Pray as you read the newspaper—visually. Many people use the paper as a prayer guide by reading a story and then verbalizing requests for the situation, which is a great way to intercede for the world. But we can expand on that by look-ing at a distressing photo and imagining (or even drawing) what the scene would look like if the kingdom of God were established in that place. If you can envision the kingdom of God, that vision can be your prayer. When you hold a new, redeemed picture in your mind (or hand), ask God to accomplish it: "Your kingdom come, your will be done on earth as it is in heaven."[193]

- Use the same technique when you walk down the street. Prayer-walking is a good start at this, but try taking it a few steps further. Notice everything that doesn't look like the kingdom of God, then picture what it *should* look like. You will begin to see kingdom possibilities wherever you go, and your prayer life will explode with renewed vision.

- If you're praying that God would bless you with a needed item (a house, a car, a garment you can't afford, and so on), draw a picture of it, and hold it close to your heart. Carry it with you wherever you go. Pray that the picture would become reality. (No, this isn't voodoo. It's a method of com-municating your thoughts that is just as valid as using words.)

- Spiritual illustrations are happening all the time in the cir-cumstances around us. Ask God to highlight some of them for you. (That's what happened when I saw a documentary about the love life of seahorses. God seemed to say, *"This is a great picture of prayer."*) Next time you see a frustrated child and feel compassion for her, God may speak to your heart: *"This is the compassion I feel when you get frustrated because you don't see the big picture."* When you see a couple excited to be with each other, you may hear him say: *"That's how I feel when I think about you."*

- For years, people have written prayer requests on slips of paper and pressed them into the cracks of the Western Wall in Jerusalem. You may not have that opportunity soon, but you can write a prayer request and stick it between the pages of your Bible, sew it into the seam of a garment, or place it under a cross displayed somewhere in your home. (Again, this isn't hocus-pocus any more than verbalizing your request is. It's a representation of what you're praying.)
- Wear colors that reflect or represent your heart's desires, frustrations, or whatever else you want to express. Tell God something like "This is how I feel" or "This is how lightly I want my circumstances to weigh on me." Wearing your prayer is an act of presenting it to God all day long, just as people in biblical times wore sackcloth to represent their grief or repentance—or as most cultures today have a color that represents mourning.
- Next time you're at the beach, write a confession or problem in the sand—a sin, a bad attitude, an obstacle to his will for your life. Ask God to bring a wave to cover it and carry it out to sea. As certainly as the waves come in, so do God's forgiveness and provisions.
- Whatever your artistic talent, use it. Draw, paint, make crafts, build models, take photographs, or do anything else you can think of to link concrete images to your inner prayers.

## Movement
- Many people walk circles around a house or building that they want to claim (in response to the Spirit's promptings) for God's kingdom, just as Israel's army marched around Jericho. If that becomes a formulaic approach for you, try

something different. But if you've never or rarely done that, why not give it a try? It's not an attempt at witchcraft, no matter what the skeptics might tell you. It's an expression of how God wants to surround dark territory with the light of his kingdom, or an acceptance of his promise to give his people the land under their feet.[194]

- Dancing is one of the most expressive things you can do with your body. Your movements can convey moods, desires, love, faith, submission, victory, and much, much more. If you envision God changing somebody or some situation as a result of your prayers, represent the change in your dance.

- When you pray for someone to be delivered from an addiction, an enslaving situation, or a destructive relationship, try making the motion of a sword cutting through the ropes that bind them or a hammer smashing the chains that weigh them down. Yes, you might look like a bad mime, but you'll express the truth of the situation accurately—and God's not judging your form.

- A variation of the above idea would be to get an actual rope or belt (à la Agabus in Acts 21:10–11), bind yourself with it to identify with the person you're praying for, and then break free in a declaration of deliverance on behalf of that person.

- If God seems distant, situate two chairs facing each other, and sit in one of them. Then picture Jesus in the other one, and have a heart-to-heart talk. By the end of the conversation, more times than not, he will seem much closer. You may even walk away from it feeling as if he has given you clear direction, though you're not quite sure how he did so without using an audible voice.

*Posture*

- Lie on your face, kneel on the floor, pace the room, spread out your hands to heaven, look up, bow down, or whatever other position may express your attitude.
- If your prayer involves denying yourself and taking up your cross, lie on a bed with your arms stretched out as if you're on a cross. Tell God you're willing to assume that position—and all it represents—in whatever situation you're praying about.
- If you're interceding for someone, try standing with your arms raised for the duration of your prayer, the way Moses did on the hill over Rephidim.[195] The tiredness you feel will remind you of the true weight of your intercession and the need for persistence. It will also illustrate how Jesus, whom Moses unwittingly depicted with his hands stretched out on a hilltop, intercedes for us.

*Sound*

- Many people listen to music when they pray. That can be calming and inspiring. But it can also be powerfully effective to sing along, speak, or shout the lyrics of a song that expresses the prayer of your heart. I once emerged from a depressing season by screaming the lyrics of "Awesome God" along with Rich Mullins, who was singing more melodiously from the CD player in my car. God's response was immediate. My discouragement vanished, and soon after, so did the difficult situation.
- If you play an instrument, come up with a melody or rhythm that first expresses your current situation, then modify it to express the solution you want God to provide

or arrange. Let your spirit offer the transition to God as an actual request.

- Some people feel that their tone of voice has to resemble a monk's whisper or Shakespearean monologue in order to qualify as real prayer. It doesn't. Nowhere does the Bible say that if you want to *be* spiritual, you have to *sound* spiritual. As with your other conversations, let your tone of voice in prayer reflect your true expression.

### *Touch*

- The biblical practices of laying hands on someone and anointing someone with oil are the two most obvious examples of prayer by touch, but there are others.
- When you pray for someone, hold his or her hands in yours—or, if the person is your spouse or a child, let every stroke or caress make an emotional statement to God about your tender care (and his) for their welfare. Take that a step further, and let your finger write or draw your request on their skin. If they need to experience God's mercy, trace "mercy"; if hope, trace "hope"; if healing or comfort, draw a cross over the place of sickness or pain.
- Touch an object used frequently by someone you're praying for (like a pillow they sleep on, a chair they sit in, and so on), and "place" God's mercies on it. Ask him to bless them whenever they touch that object.[196]
- Press a nail into your palm hard enough to hurt, but not hard enough to break the skin. Hold it there and give thanks for the cross, confessing any sins you need to confess.
- Go swimming, and as your body moves through the water,

let God wash from you the clutter of a busy life, the bad attitudes of others, and anything else that has stuck to you recently.

## Taste

- Share a meal with God. If you've partaken in the Lord's Supper, then you already have, but you can dine with him on other occasions too. We're told to "taste and see that the LORD is good."[197] There's nothing wrong with enjoying a meal as a conscious expression of our hunger for him.
- Intercede for a country by becoming physically "one" with it. Eat a Thai meal, for example, and tell him with each bite and swallow that you're eating and drinking Thailand's needs and that you identify with its people as truly as the food is becoming a part of you. Then when you bow before him, a nation bows with you.
- Jesus expected his disciples to fast, at least after he was gone.[198] Depriving yourself of taste can be a powerful prayer that expresses your desperation, repentance, grief, or spiritual focus.

## Smell

- Just because the Hindus, Buddhists, and New Agers burn incense doesn't mean God is an enemy of interesting aromas. He invented them; others simply hijack them for false religious purposes.[199]
- Confess your sins on a piece of paper, burn it in a fireplace, and smell the smoke. God is pleased with aromas of sacrifice.[200]

These are suggestions, but they barely even begin to scratch the surface. They are by no means an exhaustive list because there's no such thing. In God's creation, and with his infinite personality, expression is as diverse and creative as we want it to be. Think about it: How many ways can a creative son petition his father? A creative teenager persuade her friends? A creative salesman make a sale? A creative woman seduce a man? We demonstrate daily in human relationships that we understand creative communication. We should take every opportunity to apply that understanding to our relationship with God.

Biblical interaction with God involves taste, touch, movement, sight, smell, and sound. It's written, spoken, shouted, whispered, sung, acted out, inhaled, and eaten and tasted. It involves pleasure and pain, song and dance, art and architecture, loudness and softness, strength and gentleness, joy and grief, believing and doing—everything, including intense, passionate love. Everything the great commandment implies.

Conclusion

Esther had already spent six months being beautified by the best oils and cosmetics, and the king had already chosen her as his queen. Now an urgent situation called for a bold approach— and a creative one.

Haman, the king's right-hand man, had contrived a plot to annihilate the Jews. Esther was a Jew, and though no one in the palace knew that, she had to approach the king. That was against the law, but when you and all your relatives are about to die anyway, the prospect of punishment by death isn't much of a deterrent. So Esther called a fast among her people and prepared to meet the king.

But how? What would she do to present her request? Would she waltz into the throne room and state her business, hoping that she would be granted life long enough to get it out of her mouth? Would she appeal to the king's sense of reason and justice? Would she expose the evil plot for what it was? How would she explain her boldness?

She wouldn't, at least not yet. First she would put on her royal robes; surely the picture of her queenly attire would warm the king's heart. After all, he *had* chosen her as his favorite from the harem. He must have liked the sight of her in regal garments.

He did. As she stood in the court outside his throne room, he saw her and gave the signal to spare her life. He extended his scepter. She could proceed with her bold and creative request.

Still, Esther didn't start chatting. The king offered her up to half his kingdom, and she could have stated her business right away. But this was a marriage, not a political alliance, so she touched the top of the scepter—a gesture of gratitude and humility—and invited the king and the culprit to a banquet. She would offer her request over the comfort and generosity of a meal.

Esther pleased the king and his confidant with lavish wining and dining. Again, the doors opened wide: "What is your petition," her husband asked, "for it shall be granted to you. And what is your request? Even to half of the kingdom it shall be done."[201] Opportunities don't get much riper than this. Still, Esther deferred. Petitions require the right context and the right timing, and something told her neither was right. She invited the two to another banquet the following night.

God's timing synchronized with Esther's subtle and elaborate approach. As she was carefully cultivating a fertile environment for her petition, the Breath of God was hovering over a chaotic situation and planting his seeds of redemption within it. During the next night's banquet, Esther's request was offered, accepted, and resoundingly answered in a matter of minutes. She and her people were saved.

Creative, seductive, intimate. Like Ruth before her, Esther knew not to bring an exclusively verbal petition. Words, after all, can come across cold or presumptuous, and they offer little time for bonding. There's no ambiance with words, no opportunity for emotions to simmer in their seasonings a little longer until they're ready to be served. No, petitions depend on a proper courtship, a dance between the seeker and the sought, where royal robes and priceless perfumes can cultivate a mood. Requests are answered best in intimate moments.

*You can usually measure the depth of a relationship by the creativity that goes into it.*

You can usually measure the depth of a relationship by the creativity that goes into it. Prayer that seems lifeless and cold can only take place in an unsatisfying relationship. Prayer that dances like a celebration in Eden can only come from the Breath that moves and broods and exhales the warm Wind of life into an expressive soul. Such prayer echoes back and forth between God and those who reflect him, flourishing in the fertile garden of intimacy—where all prayers are answered. The Creator rejoices in it, and it rejoices in the Creator. It delights to be like him: imaginative, expressive, passionate, and completely enamored. And wildly, irrepressibly creative.

Notes

1. Genesis 2:3. Some translations combine these two terms, but the Hebrew text literally says "all that he created and made."
2. Genesis 1:2.
3. Francis Brown, S. R. Driver, C. A. Briggs, *A Hebrew and English Lexicon of the Old Testament* (Oxford: Clarendon, 1952), 934.
4. In both Hebrew *(ruach)* and Greek *(pneuma)*, the word for "spirit" is the same word for "wind" and "breath." Usually when a Bible translation says "spirit," in either the Old Testament or the New, the translators could just as easily have substituted the word *wind* or *breath*, and vice versa. Context determines the translators' decision in each case, but when we substitute those words interchangeably in familiar verses, we sometimes get a more powerful picture that readers of the original languages would have picked up on immediately. The text itself often seems to enjoy the interplay between these terms, a prime example being John 3:8, where Jesus tells Nicodemus, "The wind *(pneuma)* blows where it wishes and you hear the sound of it, but do not know where it comes from and where it is going; so is everyone who is born of the Spirit *(pneuma).*" In the early chapters of Genesis, the Spirit, the breath, and the wind—all from a single Hebrew word—play a prominent role. The *ruach* hovered over the deep, God exhaled his *ruach* into Adam, Adam and Eve heard God in the *ruach* of the evening ("the cool of the day"

in 3:8). Three different English translations in these passages diffuse the theme, but the original text emphasizes this "breath" of God repeatedly.

5. Genesis 4:21–22.

6. Exodus 31:1–11.

7. Hebrews 8:5.

8. Mark 10:51–52; Luke 18:40–43.

9. Matthew 9:29–30; 20:34.

10. Mark 8:22–25; John 9:1–7.

11. John 9:6–7.

12. Matthew 8:5–13.

13. Matthew 15:21–28.

14. Luke 11:42–52, for one example.

15. Mark 14:60–61; 15:4–5.

16. Hebrews 8:5 states this clearly.

17. Hebrews 10:1.

18. John 1:14.

19. Martin Kemp, ed., *Leonardo on Painting* (New Haven, CT: Yale University Press, 1989).

20. Jeremiah 1:5.

21. Psalm 139:13, NIV.

22. Romans 12:4; 1 Corinthians 12:12.

23. 1 Samuel 1.

24. 2 Samuel 6.

25. 1 Corinthians 4:16.

26. Ephesians 5:1.

27. Romans 8:29; 2 Corinthians 3:18.

28. Luke 5:30–35.

29. Romans 4:17, NIV.

30. Romans 4:18, NIV.

31. Genesis 27.

32. Many consider the story of Balak and Balaam in Numbers 22–24 to reflect the superstitions of the age. If so, the Bible portrays a naive God interacting seriously with superstition and firmly exerting his power to prevent a spoken curse. It's difficult to explain why God wouldn't just laugh them off and ignore these foolish attempts if they had no effect.

33. Proverbs 18:21.

34. James 3:5–6.

35. Matthew 12:36.

36. Romans 12:14.

37. Proverbs 4:24, NIV.

38. Matthew 15:11, NIV.

39. 1 Peter 4:11, NIV.

40. John 1:1, NIV.

41. Hebrews 1:14.

42. The Bible never refers to the occult as bogus. Its strong warnings against occult activity imply that some sort of power and effect is involved. Examples of such warnings include Leviticus 19:26; Deuteronomy 18:10–11; 1 Samuel 15:23; 28:6–20. In addition, the New Testament assumes the authenticity of occult practices and demonic activity. Examples include Mark 5:1–13; Acts 16:16; 19:18–20.

43. The "word-faith" movement is highly controversial, and with any such volatile subject, there are usually elements of truth in the middle as well as dangerous extremes at both ends of the spectrum. (In fact, there are so many gradations of this theology that it's hard to talk about it as a single movement.) Without getting into the details of this controversy, this chapter emphasizes what the Bible itself seems to say about the

power of words. To those who react negatively to the word–faith advocates, often with good reason, I'd simply urge you not to take the opposite extreme, but to seek the elements of truth that are there. After all, the opposite extreme would be to say that words aren't important and have no power at all—which essentially eliminates the need to vocally praise God or encourage a friend. On this and other issues, the right response is not the opposite of a counterfeit; it's to affirm the genuine article that the counterfeit imitates.

44. More information about Emoto's research can be found at www.hado.net.

45. Revelation 21:5.

46. Matthew 12:36.

47. Mark 1:22.

48. Matthew 8:26–27.

49. Matthew 21:19.

50. John 11:43–44.

51. John 18:6.

52. John 20:19–22.

53. See John 14:12 for a staggering example of Jesus' expectations for his disciples.

54. Mark 11:23.

55. Matthew 10:8.

56. There are several verified reports worldwide of this happening even in our day, though the verifying facts often seem to be unreasonably marginalized as fiction, depending on the predisposition of the one who assesses them. Eyewitness accounts, even those of trained physicians, are sometimes discounted simply for the assumption that resurrection "can't be true." So much for scientific objectivity.

57. Acts 3:1–10.

58. Acts 13:6–12.

59. See Ezekiel 37:1–10.

60. A few examples among many include Zaccheus climbing a tree (Luke 19:1–10), a hemorrhaging woman grabbing Jesus' prayer shawl (Matthew 9:20–22), friends of a paralytic digging a hole in the roof (Mark 2:3–5, 10–12), and a centurion who didn't even ask for a personal touch, but depended entirely on the power of Jesus' words (Matthew 8:5–10, 13).

61. Edgar Dale, *Audiovisual Methods in Teaching* (New York: Dryden Press, 1969), 108.

62. Mark 14:3–9, NIV; John 12:1–8.

63. Michael Bolton and Doug James, "How Am I Supposed to Live Without You," © 1983, April Music, Blackwood Music, and Is Hot Music.

64. Vanessa Carlton, "A Thousand Miles," © 2001 Songs of Universal, Inc. and Rosasharn Publishing.

65. Bryan Adams, Robert Lange, Michael Kamen "(Everything I Do) I Do It for You," © 1991 A&M Music.

66. Pete Ham and Tom Evans, "Without You," © 1970, 1999 Ann Marshall Herriott, Petera Ham, and Marianne Evans.

67. Michelle Branch and John Shanks, "Everywhere," © 2001 EMI Virgin Music, Line One Publishing, and Michelle Branch.

68. Jon Bon Jovi, "Always," © 1994 Polygram International Publishing and Bon Jovi Publishing.

69. Sting, "If I Ever Lose My Faith in You," © 1993 A&M Records.

70. Rob Thomas and Itaal Shur, "Smooth," © 1999 EMI-Blackwood Music (BMI), Bidnis, Inc., Itaal Shur Music.

71. Revelation 1:12, ESV.

72. Habakkuk 2:1, emphasis added.

73. Genesis 22:11, 15.

74. Genesis 15:1.

75. Genesis 18.

76. Genesis 15:8–21.

77. Genesis 12:7–8; 13:3–4, 18; 22:9.

78. Genesis 21:33.

79. Genesis 14:17–24.

80. All three of these prophetic acts can be found in Ezekiel 4–5.

81. Ezekiel 16:3–22, 30–32.

82. Matthew 13:24, NIV.

83. Matthew 13:31.

84. Matthew 13:33.

85. Matthew 13:44.

86. Matthew 13:45.

87. Matthew 13:47.

88. Matthew 18:23, NIV.

89. Matthew 20:1.

90. Matthew 22:2, NIV.

91. Matthew 25:1, NIV.

92. 1 Samuel 2:1–10, NIV.

93. Psalm 3:3–7.

94. John 11:49–52.

95. Hebrews 12:2, emphasis added.

96. Galatians 5:22–23.

97. Genesis 1:10, 12, 18, 21, 25, and 31, emphasis added.

98. The Hebrew word *tou* ("good") has emotional connotations including "delightful," "beautiful," and "precious." See *New American Standard Exhaustive Concordance of the Bible*, Robert L. Thomas ed. (Nashville: Holman, 1981) s.v.2896a.

99. Deuteronomy 28:63.

100. 1 Chronicles 29:17.

101. Psalm 51:19.

102. Proverbs 8:12, 30.

103. Proverbs 12:22.

104. Proverbs 15:8.

105. Isaiah 62:4.

106. Jeremiah 9:24.

107. Hosea 6:6.

108. Numbers 25:4.

109. Numbers 32:14.

110. Deuteronomy 9:19.

111. See Zephaniah 3:17 for one example among many.

112. John 13:23; 20:2; 21:7, 20.

113. Exodus 34:14.

114. Deuteronomy 4:24.

115. Zechariah 1:14; 8:2.

116. Deuteronomy 16:22.

117. Psalm 11:5.

118. Proverbs 6:16–19.

119. Isaiah 1:14; Amos 5:21.

120. Malachi 2:16. Contemporary Christianity cites God's hatred of divorce much more often than all his other hatreds combined, though pride, injustice, and idolatry are just as serious in his eyes. As a result, while ignoring some of our most flagrant sins, we've often unfairly portrayed the divorced as the worst of sinners. Perhaps that's because they're a much easier target than those guilty of other, more secret sins. The truth is that God hates all sin, and every human being is guilty of something God hates. But everywhere in Scripture, God's forgiveness overshadows his hatred of sin.

121. Psalm 149:4.

122. Zephaniah 3:17.

123. Matthew 8:10.

124. Luke 15:7.

125. Luke 15:22–24.

126. Matthew 23:37.

127. Ephesians 4:30.

128. 2 Kings 19:31; Isaiah 9:7; 37:32.

129. Isaiah 42:13.

130. Isaiah 59:17.

131. Ezekiel 5:13; 38:19; Zephaniah 3:8.

132. John 2:17.

133. 1 Samuel 1.

134. 2 Kings 19:1.

135. 2 Kings 20:3.

136. Hebrews 5:7.

137. Jeremiah 20:9.

138. These are admittedly unfair caricatures of monastic prayer, Puritanism, and nineteenth-century piety, all of which could be very expressive. Many medieval mystics, for example, were quite passionate in their communication with God; Jonathan Edwards, among other Puritans, wrote and spoke often about Christian "affections"; and both the pietist movement proper and early modern missionaries affected by it could be deeply (and outwardly) emotional. But the caricatures are what often impact believers today, not historical facts. Whether warranted or not, many people have a mental image of prayer as detached meditation in a stark room of a cold monastery or as a solemn, formal activity.

139. Apparently our pastor has experience in this area, particularly overseas. He once blew a shofar over the engine of a bus

that had broken down in the mountains of Peru on the way to a church service. To the complete shock of the locals— the bus driver had just identified the problem and said it would be hours before a mechanic could come and fix it— the engine fired up, and the bus made the rest of the trip with no problem.

140. It seems to me that God created images of himself when he appeared to Isaiah, Ezekiel, and Daniel; when he clothed himself in human flesh and lived among his disciples and a whole nation of Jews; and when he appeared to John in the Revelation. Not only did he allow prophets and disciples to picture him, he told them to write about what they had seen. It's impossible to read their accounts without images showing up in the mind, and it makes sense that if their insufficient words could legitimately cultivate images of God, so can our insufficient art.

141. Genesis 18:1–8.

142. Genesis 24.

143. Joshua 6.

144. Judges 6.

145. 2 Kings 5.

146. 2 Kings 13:14–19.

147. Matthew 26:7; Luke 7:37–38.

148. 1 Corinthians 14:15.

149. 1 Timothy 2:8.

150. Examples include Ezra "praying and confessing, weeping and throwing himself down before the house of God" (Ezra 10:1, NIV); Solomon "kneeling with his hands spread out toward heaven" (1 Kings 8:54, NIV); Elijah kneeling and putting his face between his knees (1 Kings 18:42); and Jesus falling "with his face to the ground" (Matthew 26:39, NIV). Jesus

also said to his disciples, "when you stand praying" (Mark 11:25, NIV). There is no dominant posture for prayer in Scripture.

151. 2 Kings 4:8–36.

152. Mark 5:38–42.

153. Ephesians 1:17–19.

154. This isn't as far-fetched or frivolous as it seems. Clothes in Scripture were a big deal. The priest wore a God-designed ephod, people put on sackcloth when they mourned, Elijah's cloak carried significant symbolism and power (1 Kings 19:19; 2 Kings 2:8, 13–14), our self-righteousness is depicted as filthy rags (Isaiah 64:6, NIV), we put on garments of salvation (Isaiah 61:10), and Jesus took off his normal clothes and wrapped himself in a servant's towel to depict his sacrifice (John 13:3–5). These were all extremely meaningful statements.

155. Isaiah 62:6–7.

156. Romans 8:26–27.

157. This was also the argument American Christians used against the radical concept of Sunday school when it crossed the Atlantic over a century ago. If anyone really wants to establish the Bible as a precise instruction manual for nonmoral issues like human expression, he or she will need to make room for someone who walks around naked for three years to make a point (Isaiah 20) or who grills his food over dung as a commentary on the nation's spiritual condition (Ezekiel 4:12–15). God didn't just tolerate acts like these, he came up with them, so we know they don't violate his character. Few in the Christian community would tolerate this sort of activity, even though it *is* found in the Bible.

158. Acts 21:10–11, NIV.

159. Acts 5:15.

160. Acts 19:11–12.

161. Genesis 30:37–42.

162. 2 Kings 2:20–21, NIV.

163. 2 Kings 6:1–6.

164. 2 Kings 4:39–41.

165. When I speak of how unnecessary it is to rigidly adhere to biblical precedents, I'm referring to modes of communication and other nonmoral issues. I'm *not* suggesting flexibility with regard to morality and ethics. Clearly, that would contradict the character of God. Diverse forms of expression, however, do not.

166. Most of his works begin with the letters J.J. for *Jesu juva*— "Jesus, help"—and end with S.D.G. for *soli deo gloria*—"for the glory of God alone." More than that, he seemed to do his work for an audience of One. One author says this about all the symbolic numbers and intricate patterns in Bach's music: "This may have been his own personal way of worshiping God. And in the end, it didn't matter if anyone else figured it all out. He was writing his music for a different audience. This was between him and the Lord." Patrick Kavanaugh, author of *Spiritual Lives of the Great Composers* (Zondervan, 1996), quoted in a column by Terry Mattingly at http://tmatt.gospelcom.net/column/2000/08/23/.

167. Maynard Solomon, *Mozart: A Life* (New York: Harper Perennial, 1996), 121.

168. Solomon, *Mozart,* 121.

169. Solomon, *Mozart,* 121.

170. Ephesians 5:1.

171. 2 Samuel 6:14–23.

172. Psalm 150:4.

173. Exodus 15:20; Psalm 30:11–12; Luke 15:25; Acts 3:7–8.

174. Many branches of Christianity in recent centuries have con-
demned dancing and denied it a legitimate role in worship.
But when the church abandons dance, we leave it in the
hands of a pagan culture. It becomes the domain of night
clubs, ballrooms, and false religions. We then define dancing
as a hypersexual mating ritual, a public exhibition of foreplay;
or perhaps as a cultic ritual of pagan religions; or as frivolous
recreation for unspiritual people who have nothing better to
do with their time. The movie *Footloose* explored this tension
between church and dance, but not fully, and not with a
very satisfying response. Many churches today, however, are
reintegrating dance into public worship, and many Christians
are reintegrating it into their private devotions.

175. Psalm 61:3.

176. Psalm 42:1.

177. Solomon, *Mozart,* 135.

178. Facts about the mating life of seahorses are taken from
"Kingdom of the Seahorse," an episode of *NOVA* that PBS
first aired on April 15, 1997. The episode focused on the
research of biologist Amanda Vincent, who spent years swimming with, tagging, and following seahorses off the coast of
Australia.

179. Ephesians 5:32, ESV.

180. John 14:2–3.

181. Ezekiel 16, quoted at length in chapter 5, is perhaps the most
graphic example of this image. But as further evidence that

words are not adequate for expressing divine thoughts—even such jolting, picturesque words as Ezekiel's—consider the life of Hosea. God had him marry a prostitute and bear children with her to illustrate his grief over Israel's adultery. Hosea didn't just write his prophecy; he had to live it.

182. Examples include commentaries on the Song of Solomon, like that of mystic Gregory of Nyssa; visions of divine marriage of Catherine of Siena, Marina d'Escobar, Angela of Foligno, Catherine of Ricci, and many others; and the ecstatic union with Jesus described by John of the Cross and Teresa of Avila.

183. Ruth 3:7, ESV.

184. Ruth 3:9, ESV.

185. 1 Kings 18.

186. Luke 1:35.

187. 1 Corinthians 15:45. Paul says in this verse that the last Adam, Jesus, became "a life-giving spirit," intentionally evoking the imagery of God's first breath into dust.

188. Song of Solomon 2:8–3:4; 5:2–8 (speaker attributions added for clarity).

189. Melody Green, "Make My Life a Prayer to You," © 1977 Melody Green.

190. Mark 12:30, compare Deuteronomy 6:5.

191. Exodus 30:34–38.

192. These are just two examples of God's precise instructions for communicating with him. Nearly every instruction for the tabernacle in Exodus and Leviticus is detailed and deliberate, not because God is finicky about every mode of expression we have—he's usually extremely open about how we speak to

him—but because these expressions pointed directly to the Messiah and his kingdom. As Hebrews 8:5 indicates, these things were a copy and shadow of heavenly realities. They had to be precise.

193. Matthew 6:10, NIV.

194. Deuteronomy 11:24.

195. Exodus 17:8–13.

196. Witchcraft counterfeits this kind of symbolic prayer by placing spells or curses on an object and expecting the spell or curse to transfer to whoever touches it. Our motive is entirely different. We utilize a physical object as a point of contact between our prayers and their needs. Unlike witchcraft, we don't expect a mechanical, impersonal cause and effect. We expect the Spirit of God to do what he wants to do in their life according to his pleasure. We act as interceders, not manipulators.

197. Psalm 34:8.

198. Matthew 6:16; 9:15.

199. This dynamic happens frequently. A God-ordained symbol or substance (incense, rainbows, the moon and stars, and so on) is twisted into meaning something it was never intended to mean, and then Christians avoid it for the meaning it falsely represents. It would be far more appropriate to reclaim God's gifts than to abandon them to counterfeit belief systems. Take them back. Use them in godly ways for godly purposes. Let your prayers rise like incense before the throne of God—literally (Revelation 8:4).

200. Exodus 29:18, 25, 41; Leviticus 4:27–31.

201. Esther 5:6.

# WAGE PRAYER

When you witness evil all around you, embrace the passionate emotion that wells up within you against Satan and his schemes. Turn your righteous anger into proactive, aggressive prayers that invite God to intervene and destroy the evil. Engage in *violent prayer*.